Leaders Under Fire

The CEO's Survival Guide to Navigating Corporate Crisis

By Jeff Chatterton & Conway Fraser

Copyright © 2020 Jeff Chatterton & Conway Fraser

All rights reserved. No part of this book may be used or reproduced in any manner whatsoever without prior written consent of the authors, except as provided by the United States of America copyright law.

Published by Best Seller Publishing®, Pasadena, CA.
Best Seller Publishing® is a registered trademark.
Printed in the United States of America.

ISBN 9798610869452

This publication is designed to provide accurate and authoritative information with regard to the subject matter covered. It is sold with the understanding that the publisher is not engaged in rendering legal, accounting, or other professional advice. If legal advice or other expert assistance is required, the services of a competent professional should be sought. The opinions expressed by the authors in this book are not endorsed by Best Seller Publishing® and are the sole responsibility of the author rendering the opinion.

For more information, please write:
Best Seller Publishing®
253 N. San Gabriel Blvd, Unit B
Pasadena, CA 91107
Visit us online at: www.BestSellerPublishing.org

Contents

About the Authors v

How to Use This Book vii

Chapter One
CEOs on the Rise 1

Chapter 2
Speed Kills Careers 15

Chapter 3
Hope Is Not a Strategy 31

Chapter 4
Do Sweat the Small Stuff 45

Chapter 5
Check Yourself Before You Wreck Yourself 61

Chapter 6
The Danger of DIY Crisis Communications 79

Chapter 7
Buckle Up and Lead—How to Navigate through the Landmines.......93

Chapter 8
The Power of a Mob..113

Chapter 9
The Aftermath..125

Conclusion 131

About the Authors

Conway Fraser and Jeff Chatterton are in the business of changing the stories people tell about you.

They left award-winning careers in journalism to help restore public reputations because they recognized that bad things happen, even to good companies. Fraser and Chatterton have crisis communication clients on six continents and have operated in many industries, including mining, tourism, construction, policing and technology.

They consider it a success when their clients **don't** make the evening news.

How to Use This Book

You're a busy person. So, we have worked hard to condense our book into a "weekend read"—information you can get through on a return flight. We have also endeavored to make this an entertaining read.

In our business, we adhere to the motto that "facts tell, but stories sell." In other words, rather than turning this into an academic-style book, it is very story driven, with lots of real-life anecdotes. In fact, the main vehicle for conveying these experiences in this book is a business parable—a fictional story of two CEOs, Bill and Raj, who are handling their crises in very different ways. We hope you will be able to place yourself into their shoes as a way to help the information truly sink in through experiential reference. We can learn from both the good and the bad.

Unless you have lived through a public relations crisis, it's hard to understand how difficult it can be to think clearly. When a story breaks, your phone is buzzing with investors, regulators, customers, employees, contractors, the general public and the media. "Chaos" is not a strong enough word. A communications crisis is something even the smartest and most experienced leaders can have difficulties managing successfully, especially if caught by surprise. When Facebook and Twitter explode with angry comments; when the TV trucks come rolling up to your door; when you have CNN on line one and the Board Chair on line two, that's when leadership is challenged and tested. Careers are made and broken during crisis.

With the evolution of 24-hour news coverage, social media, bloggers and live-streaming video applications, managing a PR crisis today is all about speed and responsiveness. In today's digital world, if you are not controlling your corporate narrative within the hour, you are accused, tried, judged, and convicted in the court of public opinion before lunch. In response, many companies procure a "crisis communications plan" from an external agency. However, we're going to show you why an "old school" crisis communications plan is giving you a false sense of security today.

The fact is crisis communications isn't an exact science. Success is usually based on lived experiences, so what we are sharing here are *our* experiences and how we approach crisis situations. Other communicators may have other approaches that work for them. This is ours. So, we're going to share PR examples of some of the crisis communications situations we have worked. However, given that we sign strict non-disclosure agreements with our clients, we have had to change names and places to ensure we respect the spirit and letter of our contractual agreements.

Our goal is to give you the philosophical fundamentals associated with being the best leader possible during a PR crisis. That means not only ensuring you have a job at the end of it but also possibly coming out of the entire situation with a better reputation than you went into it with.

CHAPTER ONE

CEOs on the Rise

Meet Bill & Raj

Bill and Raj had known each other for more than twenty years. They started their careers at the same Wall Street investment firm in New York within weeks of each other, fresh out of college. They were alike in many ways, and they thought the same way when it came to business. They had the same approach to project management and leading teams. They both looked for the opportunities in challenging situations. So, it was no surprise that they became great friends and colleagues, succeeding as a team and climbing faster than the other associates. They skyrocketed within their company and industry and quickly became the "ones to watch," but their paths soon diverged …

Climbing the Corporate Ladder

Both men had been headhunted, and one day Bill got an offer to be CEO of a blue-chip mining company. The money, stock options and career opportunities were too good to pass up, and he would also learn a new industry—mining. Raj told Bill he couldn't say no to this, even if it meant moving to Denver and seeing less of each other.

It wasn't long before Raj received a similar offer to leave the company. He was offered the CEO position at a new medical technology company called Shlomo (the name was an homage to Sigmund Schlomo Freud). Shlomo was using programmed algorithms to track mental health moods and trends, and could then connect customers with mental health professionals on demand. Raj accepted and moved his family to Boston.

Raj and Bill were realistic. Between careers, family and geography, it would be tough to stay in touch in any meaningful way—for now at least. But they had a shared retirement plan: climb fast, work hard and exit wealthy. In their respective worlds, this was a very realistic ten-year plan.

Initially, they stayed in touch regularly, thanks to technology and by having video chats at least once a month. Beyond catching up on family, they remained trusted advisors for each other. They still managed to get together in person as often as they could, but even that was tough, and soon Bill and Raj realized they hadn't met face-to-face in over a year.

Consultants and Crisis Plans

One day, a year after he started his CEO position, Bill walked into his office at a brisk pace and hit the button on his keyboard to wake up his monitor.

Raj was already waiting in the video-chat meeting room. Once the webcams synced up, Raj chuckled as he watched his friend scramble to get organized. "Hey buddy, you okay? You look stressed."

Bill shook his head in frustration. "Sorry, Raj. I was meeting with some consultants and the meeting went long."

"It happens," replied Raj. "What was the meeting about? You still working on those expansion plans for the new facility outside Carson City?"

"Unfortunately, this was a meeting with our crisis communications consultants," Bill said. "The Board said it needed to 'check some boxes' on its governance committee. They want me to have a crisis communications plan and gave me the name of someone who did a TED talk on it."

(Bill was presenting plans for a new mine to the Regional Planning Authority in Carson City, Nevada, next month; he couldn't afford anything to go sideways.)

"So, I invested and got this." With a flourish, Bill reached into his briefcase and pulled out a binder.

"What's that?" asked Raj.

"This," Bill replied, "is our brand new crisis communications plan."

"Isn't that a little primitive? A bit old school?" asked Raj.

Bill was stunned. "How is it old school? The Board is after me to brush up on crisis management. They asked me to get this done. Is there a better way?"

Raj didn't want to offend his friend. He sensed Bill's frustration and changed the subject. "Hey, did you say something about expansion plans?"

Bill's eyes popped open. He was back on territory he could get excited about. "Oh, brother, this is huge. It has the potential to move us onto the world stage. If we take over Nevada, that will make us the largest gold producer in the Western Hemisphere."

"It's looking good then?" asked Raj.

"So far, so good," admitted Bill. "I mean, things can always get thrown off at the last minute, but I'm excited at the opportunity. I've been to Carson three times in the last two weeks. I need this acquisition to happen."

What They Don't Teach in Crisis Communications
In every crisis, there is an opportunity

As Bill is already learning, defining what is and what is not a communications crisis is all about scale.

For example, companies deal with "issues" all the time, usually something that doesn't make its way into public debate or media coverage as a public relations crisis but could potentially impact the broad overall brand and reputation. An issue can be managed on an operational level and most often mitigated.

For the purpose of our discussion, a crisis of communications or PR is one that has morphed into more of an external, public issue. In this scenario, the stakes are much higher for the company and leadership. Most CEOs have experienced a crisis of some sort during their careers, but perhaps not as many have experienced one of a major scale of the type we'll review in this book.

The kind of crisis we're talking about is what *almost* happened several years ago, when we received a call about an aircraft crash in Africa. It's a tragic story, but it has a surprisingly positive ending.

It was mid-September, about one o'clock in the afternoon. The phone rang. A longstanding friend and client was on the other end of the line, and he introduced us to Nigel. Nigel owned a very unique aviation business in Africa.

Nigel was a Brit, and while you could tell he was trying to be polite, he was also on the verge of an emotional breakdown. There had been an accident earlier that morning. Details were still fuzzy, but we knew people had died. He was in the UK and was struggling to get information and figure out what was going on. He didn't know the status of the injured passengers, or the names of the deceased. All he knew was that there had been an accident, two passengers were dead, and seven more injured. He was starting to get phone calls.

We agreed to meet Nigel in Nairobi as fast as we could get there. In the meantime, we put together a holding statement to acknowledge that, yes, there had been a major incident. A holding statement is like a news release, but it doesn't say anything new. Rather, a holding statement buys time by confirming information is accurate and promising more information at a later time. The time we bought was crucial. The statement confirmed the number of passengers, deaths and injuries. It stated that the company was investigating what happened, and the owner of the company was currently en route from Europe. It also promised a further update at the end of the next business day. It wasn't perfect, but it gave us time to think. The flight to Nairobi was spent devising a strategy for Nigel and creating a laundry list of next steps (many of these next steps are things that we're going to show you in this book).

We met Nigel and immediately observed that he was in ROUGH shape. He was sleep deprived and distraught. In the time it had taken us to get to the scene, news had broken (which we anticipated), and cancellations were starting to rack up. We also predicted the hit on the business, but what we didn't expect was the scale of the impact. The company's major revenue stream had evaporated. They had lost a whopping 80 percent of bookings. Major tour operators had either suspended bookings, or cancelled completely. The local office was overrun with calls. They were fielding calls from tour operators, consumers, regulators and foreign state departments.

By the time the plane had landed, the company was effectively bankrupt. Nigel needed to communicate right away. He needed to stop the bleeding.

We sat down with Nigel and the company reps and asked a series of blunt, hard-hitting questions. It became clear that while there were unexpected winds that morning, the pilot had made a bad decision. This was not an "unfortunate incident." No, our client was responsible for the tragedy.

Pause for a second and put yourself in Nigel's shoes. You have a stressed-out group of stakeholders. You have an entire team of stressed-out employees looking to you for leadership. International headlines ensure that your phones are ringing off the hook. You've just come to terms with the fact that two people have lost their lives because of your company's conduct. Business-wise, you've lost five-million dollars in revenue in six hours. There is legitimate fear the company may not survive into the next evening.

Imagine how you would feel. It's a horrible situation to be in. When you're in that position, you have only two choices:

Option A: Accept and embrace the challenge. You just acknowledge that life is going to be rough for a while and get on with it.

Option B: Do nothing. Hide behind lawyers. Hide behind fear of saying the wrong thing. Lock the doors and don't answer accusatory media calls. We call that "turtling."

There's only one answer. You go to work on option A. So, we got to work and immediately made a few major decisions.

First: Prioritize solutions and target audiences. Don't let the media consume your resources. If you allow it, responding to media and social media can consume you. That's why it's vital to get a holding statement out immediately: it cauterizes the reputational bleeding.

We had already issued a holding statement for the media based on what we could say. Next, we decided to focus on families of the affected passengers, and travel agencies that had future bookings. We had to save the company.

At midnight, Nigel sat down with a list of priority targets. He methodically sent a personalized email or left a voicemail for everyone on that list. The message was similar to our holding statement, promising a further update by noon the next day, but this was relationship-based communication; it wasn't a mass communication. It only went to about 50 people, but it was an important 50 people. It was key to acknowledge their concerns and reassure them we were taking action.

Second: Lead with empathy. The following morning, Nigel had more information, but not enough facts to provide a meaningful update. So, we made another important decision. Our next update was not going to be a factual statement, but something even more important in these early stages: an emotional connection.

In the midst of a crisis, it's tempting to stick with the facts and only the facts. Facts are finite. Facts are something you know and can confidently report on. They become comforting in an emotionally stressful time.

But successful crisis communications isn't just about facts.

In the heat of the moment, it was important to infuse as much empathy as we could into this situation. Nigel needed to move the story away from "faceless international aviation company kills two passengers" toward "a tragic accident we feel awful about."

We helped Nigel create a communications strategy that focused on telling the truth with empathy—raw, genuine truth but mixed with a genuine intention to listen to concerns. We needed our audience to understand that we knew how they felt. We needed them to know that we knew they were scared, angry and confused. And that's all right, given the circumstances of this tragedy.

We did everything we could to "do right," and we did it with as much humanity as we could deliver.

Three: Accept responsibility when warranted. The plane crashed. And because it is the company's plane, the buck ultimately stops with them. Even if a contractor screwed up, the company hired the contractor.

Therefore, we openly admitted the company was ultimately responsible and apologized.

It wasn't a path most lawyers would have taken us down, and we knew the probability of a lawsuit was very high. But, quite frankly, we made a strategic decision. It was important that people recognized we weren't a faceless international corporation. We were a small business run by real people. If we were going to get sued anyway, we decided to try keeping damages to a minimum and try to avoid punitive damages.

Four: Less is more. We created key messages outlining the facts using plain, no-nonsense language. We admitted where we had screwed up and described the steps we were taking to ensure that it wouldn't happen again.

The beauty of succinctness is two-fold. Often, your audience is expecting you to confuse, to stammer, to avoid ugly truths. When you can come out and say, "This happened, and we feel awful about it. This is what we're going to do to prevent that from ever happening again," it's a stark contrast to what the media, the public, and even the regulators were expecting.

And being succinct means your message is much more repeatable than a long, complicated, lawyer-written statement.

Five: Be consistent and repetitive. That personal interaction kept the company alive. Enough bookings came in to keep the lights on. Nigel managed to calm the angry regulators, while doing everything he could to make life easier for the families of the affected passengers. We covered hospital bills and international travel. We arranged grief counseling and trauma counseling for the affected crew.

The company made it through the first month. And the second month.

Six: Be available. The next few days were challenging. There were raw conversations with upset families. There were awkward conversations with regulatory officials. Insurers wanted our client to shut up, and let their legal staff handle the fallout. And there were a lot of phone calls to explain what we were doing.

In our mind, it was obvious: The company had screwed up and the truth was going to come out. We made a clear and convincing argument to our insurer to let us present it on our terms. Let's keep liabilities to a minimum, let's do what's right, and let's focus on moving forward.

And a funny thing happened: Nigel started to see a light at the end of the tunnel.

Seven: Embrace opportunity. Then an *interesting* thing happened. It turns out other companies, travel agencies, even potential employees were impressed with the company's transparency and humanity through a difficult situation. They liked how it was handled. They didn't know anything about them before the accident, but they did now, and they knew that accidents happen. We left our clients with a game plan to not only continue moving forward but also find the opportunity in the situation.

A couple of years later, we were wandering the hallways of the World Travel Market in Berlin when we bumped into Nigel. This wasn't the pale, shaky Nigel we had left behind in Africa. He was happy and smiling. He had color in his face. And when he saw us, he offered to buy us a beer.

Naturally, we asked, "How's business?" Frankly, we were hoping to hear something like, "Oh, we're still doing okay. We're only down ten percent." That was a result we could live with, considering how close they came to bankruptcy.

Nigel looked relieved. The company had settled with the families out of court. The company had invested in some new technologies to prevent similar accidents in the future, and these innovations were being profiled in several trade publications. The company, despite the accident, was considered an industry leader.

"In fact, we're up 29 percent."

They grew their business precisely because of how they responded to a crisis. It was not an accident that defined them; they were defined by how they handled that accident.

They were empathetic. They were trusted. They had signed major new international clients. The regulator had approved them to fly in new markets. They had just closed the books on their highest sales month in corporate history.

Our client had fallen, but they were able to do far more than just get back to where they were. Our client had fallen up instead of fallen down. They found the opportunity in a crisis. That's what saved their reputation.

What if every crisis could yield an opportunity? What if every crisis could grow a company or improve its reputation? What if we could use a crisis to expedite zoning approvals or increase sales? What if we could use a crisis to launch new products to new markets? What if we could use a crisis to increase profitability, rather than "return to normal"?

The falling is inevitable; bad things happen. But what if rather than falling down, you could fall up? Sounds ideal, doesn't it?

Look, this isn't unheard of. In the example of Nigel, we talked about an aviation company, but it doesn't matter what sort of company you run. You can fall up.

Here's another example:

> In 1982, three people in the Chicago area died after taking contaminated Tylenol after a psychopath poisoned Tylenol bottles with cyanide. That year, Tylenol was reduced to 8 percent market share.
>
> The manufacturer, Johnson & Johnson, didn't hide. They were prompt, they were aggressive, they were empathetic, and they took action. They led with open, honest communication and new packaging technology.
>
> Throughout the 1990s and well into 2010, that number was 56 percent. That's falling up.

A crisis handled with grace and dignity is a tremendous opportunity. A crisis handled poorly will haunt you.

The opportunity lies in the fact people are talking about you. Maybe it's your existing clients and employees, but maybe it's new suppliers. New audiences/clients are going to be thinking about you for the first time in years, if they've ever heard of you at all. This is your chance. Do it right, and it's fantastic. Do it wrong and it's devastating.

The simplest way to look for an opportunity in a challenging situation is to humanize you and your company and show transparency and accountability. Again, customers, employees, politicians, the general public, and even investors understand that mistakes happen. What gives them confidence is how you handle it. Do they believe you? Do they trust you? In most cases, *that* is the opportunity available in a crisis communications situation.

Will your career be defined by getting back to normal? Normal is like a luke-warm bath: It's not bad, but it's just not good either. You can do better. You can fall up.

How to Control the Narrative 101

Regardless of the issue you're dealing with, this is the basic checklist of information you need to control the narrative and head off any possibility of looking evasive.

Address these four key questions:

1. What do we know for a fact?
2. What do we not know or can't answer?
3. What are we doing right now to fix the issue?
4. When will we have more information?

Takeaways

- Every crisis is an opportunity.
- A static crisis communications plan is a false sense of security.
- Persuading people is not just about facts.
- Lead with empathy: show them you're human.

Question to Ask Yourself: If a critical communications crisis hit your company right now, as you read this, and you were being flooded with media calls and social media posts, what is the first thing you would do?

CHAPTER 2

Speed Kills Careers

Three Weeks Later

Bill's company was under attack, and he knew he needed to take time for a phone call with his old friend, Raj.

"Thanks for taking my call on short notice," Bill said. He was out of breath. "I don't have much time, but I want to get a quick thought or two from you."

Raj replied, "I assume this has to do with Mickey Morrison tweeting about you on social media? I saw it had thousands of retweets and comments."

The activist documentarian had taken interest in Bill's gold mining company. Morrison, with six-million+ Twitter followers, had pointed to a recent environmental incident at the company's mine in Nevada in a series of tweets.

A "tailings pond" is a common mining practice of storing toxic waste sludge produced in the extraction process. In this case, the tailings pond breached its retaining walls. It came after a three-day torrential rainstorm deemed by meteorologists as a "once in a century" storm. But it wasn't the rain that did it. What followed was a minor earthquake that, combined with maximum water pressure, caused the breach. It was a couple of acts of God that may never happen at the same time again.

The "pond" was actually almost two square miles in size. When it breached, millions of gallons of the toxic waste water spilled into a river that led to a nearby lake. Cleanup crews were on the job immediately with government and environmental officials overseeing. It was serious, but not what mining professionals would deem a "crisis," given their operational approach. They would call it an "incident." But for the media and the public, it was becoming a crisis. It hadn't attracted much media coverage yet. In fact, it was almost two weeks before any media covered it. The only story at that point had been on the local radio station. The company responded by saying, "No comment."

"No Comment" *Is* a Comment

When the accident happened, Bill didn't push for a briefing. He felt it was best to let the team manage the on-site cleanup. It was several days before he truly understood what had happened. Even then, he didn't have a mining background, so he didn't understand much of the briefing.

The area was in a remote part of northern Nevada where local residents understand there were some risks associated with the mining sector. They were generally supportive because the company employed almost a thousand people in the area. The company sponsored the local minor sports leagues and even built a brand new community center. For all intents and purposes, the company was deemed a good corporate citizen.

The company didn't say anything publicly, but they notified the appropriate agencies, began cleanup, and would seek approval before restarting operations. This is mining industry protocol anywhere in the developed world. Government authorities didn't release anything either because it was only being investigated. No one had been injured, and it was far from any population. It was published online as an incident on a page buried somewhere on their website. That was about it.

Until Mickey Morrison found it and shared it with six million of his closest friends.

The Power of Celebrity Activism

Morrison started on social media from thousands of miles away. His tweet was factual and brief, and it raised questions about sustainable mining. All fair comments. The part that seemed to get the most traction was pointing out that it had happened weeks ago and had not been disclosed. Bill felt it suggested a cover-up and, truth be told, it wasn't that far off the mark. He was hoping it would go away. It wouldn't.

The corporate communications manager advised there was nothing to do. The mainstream media hadn't picked up the story … it would pass, he said. So, the company ignored it.

The next day, Bill was in a half-day meeting with his Board. When he emerged, he took his cell phone off airplane mode and it exploded like it had never done before. Emails. Texts. Social media notifications. Thousands of them. He had never experienced anything like it—a full-on air war. Some of the responses were visceral. People were calling for Bill to go to prison. Others wanted him dead. The extremity of the response was jarring, given the public didn't even have all the facts yet. What was this based on?

Bill learned the mainstream media was now tweeting, Facebooking and calling—journalists saw the incredible amount of activity the issue was getting on social media. There were comments from environmental groups, social activists, politicians and even other celebrities. Anonymous accounts were suggesting people had been killed and animals were being found dead. Other comments suggested the company had ignored engineers' advice and the tailings pond wasn't built to code. Some said the EPA was shutting the mine down. It was ludicrous. None of it was true. However, journalists were retweeting the allegations, validating them and giving them extra credibility. The media would preface the false allegations by saying, "We're looking into this." They added that there had been no comment from the company. With every passing hour, the story was being shared thousands of times. Dozens more media were calling for comment.

It got worse. The media reported some politicians were calling for Bill to be suspended pending a criminal investigation. All of this happened in four hours while Bill was in his Board meeting. He didn't know what to do. Clearly, Bill's communications manager was wrong about this being a non-issue for the media.

How could they say things so false? How does the company stop these people? Can we sue? The panicked questions rifled through Bill's mind like machine gun fire. The feeling of powerlessness was crippling.

False Sense of Security

Bill updated Raj on all this. But then he asked the question Raj wasn't comfortable with. "Look, Raj, on our last call, when I mentioned I had a new crisis communications plan, I know you weren't comfortable. What's going on?"

Raj shifted in his seat. He didn't want to offend his friend, but he was asked a direct question. "A crisis plan may have worked well a decade ago, but the game has changed. The world is faster, so we feel it's more effective to outsource our crisis advice. We engage an expert, who's great. She understands modern crisis communications far better than we ever could."

He continued, "I looked at the crisis consultants. They all promise a customized plan, but when you delve deep and compare entire sections at random, they more or less say the same thing. I just didn't want to pay a massive premium to get regurgitated boilerplate stuff. We needed the folks who could deliver a result, not a process. It's also nice to have an outsider's perspective ... a fresh lens."

Bill was coming to a sad, shocking conclusion. Despite having spent all that money and investing all that time, his crisis communications plan was useless. There wasn't a section dedicated to "celebrity activism." He had no idea what to do next and hoped Raj could offer some clarity and insights to save the day.

Yet, Raj didn't know what to say because he had never experienced anything like this either. Raj realized that not only was his best friend in a lot of trouble, he was also vulnerable.

"Bill, you need to go to your Board Chair right away with an update on the media onslaught," Raj suggested. "If I remember, your Chair has been in the mining business 40 years. He likely has connections or insight. Don't waste another moment. When push comes to shove, if this gets worse, you're going to need the support of the Board. Focus there for now."

Bill agreed. It turned out to be great advice because the company's problems were only beginning.

Preparing for the Worst

Do you know anyone who has experienced the kind of attack Bill faced? Have you ever felt it? It feels like drowning without being in water. It is like being attacked by a swarm of bees without actually being stung. If you haven't worked up a tolerance to it and don't know what to expect, it can leave you immobilized.

What Bill is experiencing in our story is raw reality. It happens every day. The speed of a news cycle is unlike anything you have ever seen unless you have been in the middle of it. It is a storm of storms—a mob-rule mentality. Truth and context are irrelevant when emotion and moral objection jump in the way.

"No comment" is, therefore, not an option. If you don't tell your own narrative, someone else will tell it for you. The media and the public associates "no comment" with being guilty or hiding something. Journalists are in a highly competitive profession dictated by ruthless deadlines and the need to get people "on the record." Not feeding that beast simply means you'll anger it and it will go get food somewhere else … and it won't end well for you.

There are a few things to remember when shit hits the fan.

1. There's a race to get it first, not to get it right.

We recently had a client experience an on-site explosion in a vacant building. Someone took a photo of it and shared it on Twitter. The photo was retweeted by local media and then seen by national media. All this happened inside 30 minutes. A decade ago, the company would have had hours to prepare a response. Not anymore.

The media didn't even call the company to verify what happened. Social media took off like wildfire. The photo was much more dramatic than the reality of the situation because the photographer applied a dramatic and ominous filter which made the fire look much worse, like something out of an apocalyptic movie.

Within an hour, the company clarified the situation, distributed a true, unfiltered photo, reported no injuries and the story went away. We were able to convince the media they had been manipulated and they agreed to run a correction and an apology. However, not everyone sees the apology. The reputational damage had been done.

2. Tell them *something*.

Even when you can't get ahead of the story, avoid a "no comment" response. You might as well run to the top of the mountain to scream, "We're guilty!"

You don't have to give away the farm or talk about things you don't have enough information on. But there are ways to eloquently spend a minute talking and not expose yourself.

For example, in Bill's situation, when the media called, he could have said something like:

> "We did have a tailings pond breach after record rainfall and an earthquake. The proper officials were notified right away and are on scene right now monitoring the cleanup. We are assisting them in any way they direct us to. The site is stabilized, and our employees are already back to work. Now we're focusing on assessing any impact and ensuring it never happens again. When we have more information, we'll be releasing that to the public. Beyond that, there's not much else we can share at this time."

It's factual. It's not groundbreaking information, but enough to ensure you're present in the story and not saying "no comment."

What we know is the only way to survive with your reputation in place and a job in tact is to get ahead of the mob with a rapid response. Own your narrative.

What is a rapid response? Rapid response means minutes, not hours. If you don't reply quickly, the media and social media mob will fill the void with rumour and speculation. The media will also question your motives if you're being evasive.

You don't need all the answers. What you do need are the basic facts. You may need as little as a few sentences to confirm basic facts and communicate that you are in control of the situation. If there's a story, the media will tell it with or without you. If you don't respond, it means more airtime or column space for those who will condemn you.

We won't demonize the media. Journalists are committed to telling stories that impact people. So, in a crisis situation, be a part of the solution. View them as an opportunity. Going through the mainstream media is still the fastest way to get your side of the story out to the most people possible. Media outlets and reporters have the largest social media followings. Will you get asked tough questions? Absolutely. It's your job to be ready for those questions.

Long before a crisis happens, you should be thoroughly media-trained. We anticipate crisis situations and grill our clients with mock interviews. We hammer them hard with difficult questions and hypothetical situations, and we do it multiple times so that when the real thing happens, they are ready for anything.

3. Accept that life isn't fair.

Once the story is shared or aired, yes, much of what will be said about you and your company on social media will be mean and often incorrect. Come to terms with the fact that life isn't fair and the world is mean. Your job is to work within that reality.

Never has the threat of media hype been more relevant than it is today. Social media channels draw huge audiences where no one seems to be bound by things like facts, due process or journalistic balance.

Today, you are guilty until proven innocent in the court of public opinion. There is a heavy sentence for those the mob deems guilty. Everyone is a reporter today. Everyone is a broadcaster with huge audiences. And, everyone wants their social post or tweet to go viral. So, the more sensational, the better.

"It takes many good deeds to build a good reputation, and only one bad one to lose it."

Benjamin Franklin wrote those words more than 300 years ago when news traveled more slowly. But even back then people understood the fragility of a reputation and the value of protecting it. Little did they know how communication would evolve between then and now. You see, humans screw up. But these days, in the Orwellian Big-Brother society we live in, one mistake, like discussing something very private in public, can lead to the end of a reputation, relationship or career.

Ten years ago, the only way to broadcast an event live was with a broadcast satellite truck. Today, everyone has a mobile recording device (their phone) and the ability to broadcast what they see and hear to a global audience instantaneously. They have platforms like Facebook, Twitter, Instagram, Snapchat, YouTube, blogs, etc. These "reporters" can be six-year-olds with an iPad or 86-year-olds with a mobile phone. And, once they share what they see, hear or record, their followers then share it to their friends, and so on, and so on. Social media is the largest water cooler in the world …

… and it's a water cooler that can flood a boardroom.

4. Fewer journalists doing more = more mistakes.

What is new to journalism is how social media is impacting mainstream media. Journalists struggle to stay relevant in a social media world where the emphasis is getting it first over getting it right. Through declining media advertising sales and subscriptions, media outlets are treading water, and that has meant reductions in newsroom staff and chasing sensational stories over ones with greater-good value. A recent journalism census by the American Society of Newsroom Editors reported a 10 percent decrease in U.S. journalists in a single year. As Ken Doctor, author of *Newsonomics: Twelve New Trends That Will Shape the News You Get*, points out, the number of professional journalists in the U.S. today is about half of what it was 25 years ago and dropping fast. It's a global trend.

Not only do we have fewer journalists, but those journalists still working are being asked to do more with less. They're writing more stories each day, and that means less time for research and sourcing. They're also having to blog and post to social media. Print reporters have to take care of their own photography and videography in many cases, too. While they're doing all this, they're not 100 percent focused on their journalism, which involves both listening and asking tough questions. Whether they admit it or not, it's impacting the quality of work. There are more mistakes making it into the media. Journalists aren't happy about this, but they have no choice; this is their new reality. We are a lesser society with fewer professional journalists who have the time to do proper research.

Prepare for the Oncoming Storm

So, what does this mean for you? It means that, more than ever, you and your company need to communicate quickly and in language the media will understand. Will regular people understand what you're saying or are you speaking in technical jargon? Don't consider using plain English "dumbing down"; it's about clarity for the purposes of protecting your reputation.

Make the journalist's job as easy as possible in getting your side of the story accurate. If you do an interview, you could even follow up by emailing the reporter a one-page fact sheet to clarify all your main points. Ensure you can reference the sources for the facts you're sharing.

Unfortunately, there are no signs of it getting better. Many younger journalists who have come up in a "star culture" of "infotainment" aspire to get a blue check mark beside their Twitter name and to be a guest on a popular podcast. Some are not interested in spending countless hours slogging through corporate documents. An indicator of this change is how many college journalism programs around the world have completely folded in recent years. They're reacting to the fact there are fewer journalism jobs at the local and regional levels (where most entry-level journalists get their start). However, when educational institutions start closing journalism programs, they are, in effect, saying there is no future in this profession, which is quite the declaration to the next generation of leaders and influencers.

So, why should you care as an executive?

Well, these are the young people who are driving the public narrative, and you're not prepared for it. The truth and context have become unfortunate victims of this race for supremacy. In other words, it's a jungle out there, and it's a bad place to be if you're the hunted, like the leader of a company in trouble. You see, in every good news story there's a hero and a villain—or perhaps a victim and a villain. Ask yourself when you last saw a story in which the company or the CEO was the hero or the victim. This is the reality of the reputation wars today, and CEOs are losing.

5. The cover-up is usually worse than the blunder.

Look at data privacy breaches. It happens so often now that people have come to accept the privacy risks associated with the convenience of technology. Yet when companies experience a data breach, they tend to keep it quiet. Ultimately, someone finds out, it is reported and the reputation of the company takes a hit. Maybe it is not an instant kill shot, but rather a slow reputational death by a thousand cuts.

Look at Google. There was a massive data breach in 2018 and 500,000 accounts were exposed to over 400 third-party applications. But that's not why they got heat. No, Google got hammered over sitting on the privacy breach for almost seven months before the *Wall Street Journal* exposed it to the world.

Ask Apple. It was exposed for creating software updates that slowed down older iPhone models, forcing people to buy new phones. It was the latest of many PR blunders for Apple that strikes at the very anti-establishment brand Steve Jobs fought to build. It all adds up.

Facebook has lived this nightmare after trying to hide the fact it harvested tens of millions of Facebook profiles for the political consultancy firm Cambridge Analytica. It ended with CEO Mark Zuckerberg facing a grilling at a U.S. Senate hearing.

Uber is part of this fraternity as well. It tried to cover up a data breach, and it cost them $148 million in penalties. Uber wasn't being deliberate in the data breach; it was hacked. It was a victim.

Even though you're not overtly lying, when you cover something up or fail to disclose something, it is perceived as being dishonest. And, in our line of business, we have a non-negotiable philosophy: NEVER LIE. The lie is usually worse than the actual infraction and near impossible for a leader to recover from.

6. If you're defending, you're losing.

The fact is, in the court of public opinion, if you are defending you are losing. Period. Defending is being defensive.

Our rule is pretty simple: if you believe there is a reasonable chance an incident will become public at some point, it is always best to get ahead of the story and dictate the narrative yourself. So, how do you do that?

Know your message. Now, we are not suggesting getting ahead of a story will ensure a pain-free process. What getting ahead of a story does is increases the probability of overall long-term reputational success. The devil is in the details when it comes to knowing your message, your target audience, anticipating challenging questions and how to answer them, and doing enough preparation that you're confident when you go public.

The key benefit is that you set the narrative. So, for example, let's pretend we own Google. Instead of a story about how Google hides important details, let's rewrite the narrative. Let's tell the story about how Google is the most transparent mega-company (way better than Facebook and Uber). Google is one of the most secure tech companies in the world and invests billions in privacy research and development each year to keep information safe. Even when hackers do get through, Google shuts it down fast and experts learn how to ensure your information is more secure than ever.

Timing is everything. Another substantial benefit to proactively communicating a potentially negative story is that it allows you to control when the story is made public—a huge strategic advantage. A typical example means releasing something on the Friday of a long weekend so that it gets lost in the domestic chaos of a holiday weekend.

Getting ahead of the story also allows your communications professionals and lawyers to collaborate on messaging that ensures you are protected in both the court of law and the court of public opinion.

Sometimes it's better to self-inflict an inevitable wound if you can ensure it won't be lethal. You can't undo what has happened; what you *can* control is whether you are perceived as honest, open and transparent.

Stand your ground. We will warn you now: In your boardroom, this will be an unpopular opinion for some. Maybe your Board Chair, maybe some VPs and very possibly your lawyer will all have different experience, understanding and agendas. Your job as a leader is to convince them that if there's no avoiding this story, it's best to get ahead and own it. Remember, the company will survive, but it's your personal reputation on the line.

People will forgive something going wrong because, hey, shit happens. But they can't forget that feeling when they found out you weren't honest about it with them. It calls everything you do after that into question in their minds. You can't undo that feeling.

In our parable, Bill did not adhere to this philosophy, more out of ignorance than arrogance, and he's paying for it already. When you look at Bill's situation, he and his team did not focus on getting ahead of the story. They weren't solution-driven. Instead, their plan was to hope it would not become a public issue.

Plan for the worst and hope for the best.

Five Ways to Piss Off a Reporter

Do any of these things to a reporter, and you're in for a world of hurt:

1. **Tell reporters how to do their job**—they love that they love that (please apply appropriate level of sarcasm in this section). Criticize the subjective tone or focus of a story while you're at it. Bonus points if you can do this while never mentioning that the story was technically 100 percent accurate.

2. **Ask them why they didn't cover your story.** Reporters love justifying how they do their job and the decisions they've made to PR people. If you ask with a little bit of attitude, all the better.

3. **Only be helpful when you want something from them**. Reporters can't tell when they have an artificial one-way relationship with a PR person. No need in investing a little time in getting to know them and *their* needs.

4. **Send them a media advisory *right* before an event**. They will never guess that you don't want them there and made it logistically impossible for them to get there on time without being able to say they weren't invited.

5. **Only communicate with them by email or text.** Reporters love nothing more than a controlled message via email with no chance to ask a question. Sometimes you have no choice—but we're talking about the other 99 percent of the time. An email is great for communicating tone, too.

Takeaways

- Focus on a solution.
- Speed kills. Prepare for rapid response.
- Get ahead of the story. Own your narrative.
- "No comment" is a comment (and not a good one).
- Never lie. It does irreversible damage.

Questions to Ask Yourself: If a crisis happened right now, who would do the interviews at the media conference? Who is that person's backup if you can't reach them?

CHAPTER 3

Hope Is Not a Strategy

One Week Later

Raj leaned back at his desk, staring at the ceiling. He hung up the phone with Carrie Boswick, his crisis communication consultant.

Crisis was nothing new to Carrie. Her husband often joked that he married a firefighter. She had started as a reporter, straight out of school. After a few years working in Des Moines, she was promoted to Chicago, where she had won an industry award for her work as an investigative reporter. She left journalism around her 40th birthday to work for a pro-business lobbying group communicating with politicians in Washington DC. After five years of high-stakes political gamesmanship, she was poached by the Bavington team.

She had been there and done that. Now in her late 40s, Carrie had lots of hands-on experience when reputations and businesses were on the line. She often joked that her facial wrinkles were the road map of experience. She was sardonic and sassy.

The Bavington Group had a reputation for being very good. But Raj was initially sceptical about bringing them on board—they were expensive, after all. What sold him, ultimately, was their "insurance" program. Rather unique to the industry, Raj paid a flat monthly rate, which gave him access to Carrie and her team whenever he needed her. It was a relief knowing a crisis team that knew his company, his issues and his media environment was on permanent standby. It was even *more* of a relief knowing that if he *did* have to make a call, he wasn't going to get dinged by huge fees with consultants who were charging an hourly rate.

This time, the "crisis" was a minor issue with some data-flow issues. People were signing up for the app but then complaining they didn't have access. Raj knew it might be an issue with a server at a data centre in California and had called Carrie so that she was briefed.

As he got up to wander down the hall, it occurred to him how much more focused he was these days. A few months previously, a server error would have set off a series of chaotic events. It would have tied him up for hours making frantic phone calls with lab technicians, supervisors and Vice Presidents. Then they'd sit in fear, waiting for a phone call from nosy reporters. As a growing company, Shlomo could not afford negative publicity.

This time around, he sent one email to his Regional VP that said, "Tell me what you need to do to fix it. Let me know if it attracts attention." Raj was confident that if things did become public, Carrie would help him through it and he could get on with fixing the next problem. It was liberating.

Meanwhile, in Denver...

Bill was sitting at his desk rubbing his temples. The headache hadn't gone away in days, and it hung there, like a constant reminder that his days were a steady stream of challenges, a metaphorical headache that wouldn't disappear. He was tired, he was irritable.

The tailings pond had breached its retaining wall close to three weeks ago. He thought he'd be able to send in a few reports to the Environmental Protection Agency and be done with things by now. He was wrong. After Mickey Morrison pointed out the issue on Twitter, the phone calls, emails and harassment would not go away.

Bill was sitting with Todd, the company's in-house lawyer, and Nicholas, the Chair of the Board of Directors. The three were discussing an especially difficult reporter.

"He's not going away," said Bill. "We issued a news release, like the plan said, but all that did was make him ask a lot of questions. First, it was about the engineering reports. Now he's asking questions about long-term health effects. He wants to sit down this afternoon and do an interview. I imagine he wants to know what we're doing to prevent similar accidents at our other facilities."

That set off a furious discussion amongst the men. There were simply too many unknowns to do an interview: They didn't have full results back from some water testing; they were running other tests on toxins; and they had inspectors from the EPA who were still on the scene.

Bill felt his headache get a bit worse. "Look, they're killing us here. This reporter has a bone in his jaws, and he's not going to let go."

Todd, the lawyer, looked back at his CEO, staring at him through his thick glasses. "That's why you can't take the bait. He is going to have to wait. We don't have enough information yet. We don't know why the wall failed, and we don't know what the impacts are. The minute we have better knowledge, we can talk to people, but it's *way* too early to talk about remediation or next steps! I mean, if we talk to him now, he'll be calling on a massive groundwater cleanup campaign that could cost the company millions of dollars."

Bill thought he could plead his case. "Let's talk about the work we've put into cleaning it up since the accident."

"Absolutely not!" Todd exploded. "If we say the wrong thing right now, it could cost us a fortune in legal settlements. I can't let you expose us to that kind of legal liability."

The three of them discussed this point for the next fifteen minutes. Bill felt the company could highlight the steps it was taking to make things right. The lawyer felt that by talking about "making things right," it would merely accentuate that the company had been doing things wrong.

It was a sticky point, and the disagreement was getting louder.

"Come *on*, guys." Bill went back to rubbing his temples. "This is bullshit! We're trying to do the right thing here, are we not? I'm getting sick and tired of being crucified for not answering his questions. Can't we come up with something that answers his questions without exposing ourselves to further liability?"

"No," replied the company lawyer. "Here's the problem. I know you want to talk about our cleanup, but right now we don't know *exactly* what we're cleaning up. We don't know what happened and we don't know what we're going to do to fix it. We don't know how bad the damage is. We don't know how much it's going to cost. We don't even know if the breach is our responsibility and if it's not our responsibility, we sure shouldn't be talking about it."

Nicholas, the Board Chair, was oddly quiet throughout the conversation. He leaned back and observed the two of them, content to let the lawyer and CEO duke it out over proper strategy.

Eventually, Bill shook his head in sad resignation. The company lawyer and Board Chair left him with his thoughts. Bill tried to ignore the headache, and walked back to his computer. He hit refresh on the local news page and cursed. The online edition of the local newspaper had a new top headline: Local Mining Executive Refuses to Answer Questions about Safety Record.

Bill was pissed. His headache was twice as strong. As he scanned the article, his mood worsened still … the article was full of some damning evidence and statistics, and half of those statistics were factually incorrect.

"For the love of God," Bill muttered under his breath.

Lawyers aren't communication professionals.

Compounding the problem for Bill and the Board was the advice they were getting from their corporate lawyer: say nothing. "If we say nothing," the lawyer said, "we can't get in legal trouble and we're not sure where this is going with the regulatory bodies." This was extremely poor PR advice but not uncommon in the corporate world. It may be sound legal advice; however, in the court of public opinion, saying nothing is associated with hiding something and being guilty.

Don't depend on your lawyer for communications advice. Although valuable members of the corporate team, lawyers defend companies in a court of law where the rules are clear, and the wheels move slowly … very slowly. From a lawyer's perspective, the more you say, the more risk you accept.

While that may be true in a court of law, silence in the court of public opinion is deadly. In that court, there are no rules, justice is levelled at lightspeed and judgments are based on limited, inaccurate information. In the court of public opinion, sentences can be career ending.

Say something, but don't infer guilt.

We get it: lawyers don't want you to harm yourself. But rather than making "no comment" the default position, put in some effort. Find a way to say *something*, even if that something is an explanation of why you can't say more.

It is important to remember that lawyers work for companies and not CEOs. Like Boards, their fiduciary duty is to the company and the company only. CEOs come and go.

The Story of Greg: A Classic Scapegoat

Sooner or later, the overwhelming majority of companies and/or CEOs experience a communications crisis of varying degrees. The sooner you accept the inevitable, you'll be better off in the long run.

In Chapter 2, we told you the story about an aviation company that grew 29 percent after a fatal accident. Let us tell you a similar story about a similar accident, but with a very different outcome for our client. This is the story of Greg, a CEO of another air charter company that simply wasn't prepared for a crisis, and it cost him almost everything. In our first story, our client owned the company outright. It's hard to fire an owner, but it's easy to fire a mere senior leader. If you're a food manufacturer, you need to know what to do in the event of a food recall. If you're a mining company, you should know what to do when a tailings pond spills. If you're a tech company, you should be prepared for a massive data breach …

… and if you're a charter airline, you should be prepared for what to do in the event of a fatal accident. Greg was not prepared.

We got Greg's call two hours after a Cessna Caravan had gone down, killing eleven people. His call to us was brief, emotional and frantic. Greg was both despondent and in full-on panic mode. The plane was literally still smoking, and he was scrambling to figure out what to do next. We were able to help him identify the immediate next steps, but the clock was ticking. He and his staff were distraught, confused, and the phone started to ring.

In the event of a crisis, there is a lot to do. We got the media statement out and had it on their website within minutes. But we also had to scramble to get a lot of stuff done that should have (and could have) been identified in advance.

- ➢ We walked them through how to notify the families. There are good ways to do that and there are horrible ways to do that. Unfortunately, Greg and his team had to figure this all out on the fly.
- ➢ We put together messages for frontline telephone staff. Anxious passengers were calling, wondering if their scheduled flight would still go ahead. Greg hadn't considered what impact a fatal accident would have on his current bookings.
- ➢ We created messaging for concerned family members of passengers that were *not* affected. When one plane went down, there were multiple scheduled flights that were still in the air.
- ➢ Logistically, Greg was scrambling to figure out exactly *who* to notify at the different regulatory authorities. Greg had regular contact information for a lot of people, but there was no clearly identified list of exactly who to contact and how to find them.
- ➢ Greg was also scrambling to secure the scene, which has a bunch of challenges that not every company will deal with.

Greg was grieving, he wasn't thinking straight, and he was desperately trying to avoid making a mistake. In the meantime, his staff were frantic and distraught. Many of the senior managers were friends with the pilot who had gone down.

But even though they were doing nothing right from an operations perspective, the company survived. How?

What saved the day for the company?

The operations were a mess, so what saved the company? Their communications were fine. Greg was able to communicate quickly, honestly, with transparency and empathy to all the right audiences, right away.

They had some key crisis protocols in place with some strong external third-party external support and they understood the importance of acting quickly.

As it turns out, the company had suffered a very visible, non-fatal accident only five weeks earlier. While there were only minor injuries, the plane was badly damaged. Pictures of the crashed plane had been in the news. That accident was still fresh in customers' minds.

That's toxic. That's a double-whammy of bad messaging. If a picture is worth a thousand words, the follow up to that proverb should be "and two pictures, spaced only a few weeks apart, multiply each other." A thousand times a thousand. The emotional impact of seeing this accident is worth a million words.

> *In late October, 2018, Lion Air 610 crashed into the sea off the Indonesian coast. The plane was a newly designed Boeing 737 MAX 8. It was a tragedy, but the collective world shrugged. That was until March 2019, when another MAX 8 jet crashed in Ethiopia. The 1-2 punch that Boeing suffered was massive. Every MAX series jet was grounded. A single airline accident in and of itself is a problem, but two accidents in close proximity is absolutely toxic.*

This means any "traditional" messaging you use after an airplane crashed would be useless. Key takeaway is there are some things that you can't prepare for. However, that doesn't excuse a lack of preparation on the things you *can* prepare for.

A Simple Survival Plan

Our survival plan was simple: We had to be nimble, be responsive, and communicate. We had to communicate with authenticity and honesty. You can't communicate authentically if you're using canned messages, so that "What to say if our airplane crashes" section of your binder would have been entirely useless.

You can't communicate authentically using a canned message. So, we got to work. And we communicated, with openness and honesty.

We created empathy-laden messages. We followed a game plan that was very similar to the accident we discussed in chapter two, and we shared everything we could legally say about the accident. And if there were things we couldn't say, we talked about why we couldn't share them.

We figured out who we needed to talk to. We prioritized our communication and focused on families, existing customers and future customers. We put together an email newsletter that outlined steps we were taking every day. We committed to do everything we could to prevent this from ever happening again. And over the next several days, weeks and months, we communicated our progress.

Being that transparent involved a culture shift. Transparency led to heated debates, but in the end, it was simple: Being open and transparent was our only way forward. It was the right thing to do.

Did it work? It was a mixed bag. For the company, it worked, absolutely. We were able to shore up our nervous industrial suppliers and clients. Sales took a short-term hit, but quickly bounced back to pre-accident levels. The families were cared for. Life returned to a new, open, authentic normal.

Consider the Short-Term Price

The short-term price was that Greg had to step down as CEO. He lasted about five weeks after the accident and was then reassigned. And yes, you can bet that when he was reassigned, we used his departure as a way of signalling a turning of the page and a new safety-oriented culture.

Their communications were fantastic. Those communications were able to save the company, but they couldn't save Greg's career.

Brainstorm Worst-Case Scenarios

Something bad will eventually happen. And when it happens, it's going to be stark, it's going to be scary, and it will either make or break your career. Take a look over the past several decades. If you're a large electrical utility, you can prepare for power outages. But look at what hurt Pacific Gas and Electric (PG&E) in California … it wasn't power outages, or utility rates, or political squabbling over renewable energy. The issue that knocked PG&E down was a feisty advocate named Erin Brockovich. Her claim that an entire community had cancer was a poignant story. The Erin Brockovich story was so poignant it became a major motion picture with Julia Roberts playing the antagonist.

If you're a consumer goods manufacturer like Samsung, you may prepare for product recalls. You might prepare for health concerns related to radiation, and competition from Apple. But I bet there's no chapter in their crisis manual about "What to do when our phones catch fire and are banned from every airplane in the world." The Note 7 phone recall was big, it was ugly, and it cost several people their hard-earned careers. Similarly, if you're Toyota, you may prepare for warranty issues and sporadic recalls, but there are very few playbooks for what happens when you're the subject of the largest recall in US history.

These crisis situations are no different than having a fire. You can't fully plan for a fire, but you can have protocols in place. And even when that big fire breaks out, you call the fire department—you won't try extinguishing it yourself. So, why is that any different in a reputational crisis? Call a specialist.

That ability to recognize a bad play and change on the fly does not come easily. It comes with experience and expertise. It requires a neutral party who is not emotionally involved in the crisis. It is very difficult to be dispassionate when it's your career on the line. It's impossible to think clearly when your pulse is doing 120 beats per minute and your mouth is dry.

Enlist a Trusted Third Party

This is when you, as a leader, need that trusted third party. You need that voice on the other end of the line who can restore some sanity during a frantic time. You need the ability to think calmly, clearly and unemotionally. That voice is worth millions of dollars to you at that time.

There are many good crisis communications people out there. You just need to do your research and establish that connection ahead of time to ensure they're ready to move fast when you need them.

Hope is not a strategy. Hope is gambling. And gambling is dangerous.

Five Signs Your Crisis Consultant May Not Be Right For You

1. They charge hourly.

Stop and think about this. Would you rather pay someone $200 an hour to go through five hours of pain, or pay someone $1,000 and go through 30 minutes of pain? Crisis teams that charge you a project rate are incentivized to make the problem go away as quickly as possible. That's a win-win. If your crisis consultant quotes you an hourly rate, walk away. You should never incentivize stalling on a solution. Quick, dirty and done is always going to be better than perfect, pretty and painful.

2. They have logos on their website.

Take a look at your crisis consultant's corporate website. Is it full of Fortune 500 company logos while bragging about the work they've done for those firms? A few things to note: Doing a one-day training program for a satellite office of a Fortune 500 is not the same thing as "working with them." Furthermore, do you want your logo up there? Your crisis team should be there to shut down and resolve the worst day of your life … not brag about it.

3. Crisis is an add-on.

Does your crisis communications team do public affairs, government relations, digital marketing, graphic design, websites and integrated marketing? Crisis communications is the outlier and outsider of the communications family. Your reputation doesn't deserve generalist treatment. On the worst day of your corporate life, go straight to the specialists.

4. They don't have wrinkles.

That's actually a good thing. Crisis is stressful, but it gets easier to manage with experience. If your marketing agency sends over a 25-year-old to handle your corporate crisis, it's time to ask some tough questions about experience. Wrinkles and gray hair are a good thing. This is an experience-based sector that allows for rapid response and decisive counsel.

5. They don't have newsroom experience.

Even if your crisis isn't media related, a newsroom is an absolute pressure cooker (see point 4 about wrinkles). There are very few corporate incubators that can recreate the stress of crisis communications better than the day-to-day chaos of a newsroom. Reporters have seen all the tricks, they know what works and what will fail. Use that experience to your advantage.

Takeaways

- Prepare for the worst. Hope is not a plan.
- Companies survive crisis. CEOs often do not if unprepared.
- The most dangerous questions in a crisis are "how" and "why."

Questions to Ask Yourself: When a crisis hits, where will your off-site "war room" be for centralizing the communications process? What communications tools will be in the war room (i.e., landline, good wifi, printer, contact list, and so on)?

CHAPTER 4

Do Sweat the Small Stuff

One Week Later

"Sorry I'm late," Raj said to Bill.

Raj despised it when people were late for meetings, so he recognized the inconvenience.

"I'm on break from a full-day media coaching session our consultants set up," he said as he got settled in for their video call.

Media coaching was one of those things people like Bill and Raj always joked about, calling them "soft skills." Back in the early days at the financial firm, they were both considered the best communicators of all the associates. Charming and quick-witted, both had the ability to get a point across and hold people's attention during a meeting. When the *Wall Street Journal* was doing a feature on the next generation of leaders, their then-Director recommended Bill and Raj as interviewees. It was a great experience and a huge ego boost. The questions were softballs for the most part. Bill actually had his printed interview framed and hung on the wall of his office like a trophy fish.

"Why are you getting media coaching?" Bill asked.

Raj explained it had actually been set up months ago for him and three other senior executives. The hard part was scheduling everyone to be available on the same day. But, it was a priority. The strategic advice Raj got was that they needed to build some capacity for a rainy day. With the media being so hurried and overworked these days, it was more important than ever to be able to deliver a clear, concise message. They needed to be strategic.

They were planning an outreach tour. Raj and his Chief Innovation Officer were going to spend a week traveling the country. They would meet with specific health and tech influencers, as well as other key journalistic influencers. There would be sit-downs with mental health associations, regulators and the investment community. No scheduled interviews, no pitch; only meetings. Like most successful business leaders, Raj knew the best time to meet someone was when you did not want anything from them.

Would Have, Should Have, Could Have

Bill listened to what Raj had done and had trouble processing the strategy. It was not that he disagreed, but he was in a different headspace than Raj at the moment.

"That makes sense," Bill interjected. "I should have done that. It would have helped right now with this attack on social media and the media. I am completely overwhelmed."

Bill realized mining communications has been doing it wrong all along. The isolated bunker mentality wasn't working. He had never done any proactive work with media and had never taken meetings with stakeholders like the Indigenous Environmental Alliance, the Sierra Club and Environment America. In fairness, he works for a mining company and mining companies always begin from the position of being the "bad guy." However, meeting with the groups proactively would let them meet Bill, get to know the person, what his belief systems are, and what he is doing to try to mine sustainably. That's something. And something is better than nothing.

Instead, most of the focus was on investors and contractors. It's important work. However, so was having a handle on public opinion. Relationship-building hadn't been a focus, and he was realizing he was paying for that in times of crisis. Public opinion was turning hard on the gold mining company, and that was impacting the markets. Bill also got the sense trouble was brewing with politicians. He wasn't thinking of communications as a "soft skill" any longer.

"How are you finding the media coaching, Raj?" Bill asked, now sensing there was a huge hole in his leadership game.

Raj responded, "You start to realize there is a real art to communicating. The nonverbal communication piece is a true art—things like body language and tone of voice. And then there are ways to develop a main message, knowing your target audience, and how to pivot away from difficult questions." He continued, "And, I can see how it will help me, even outside media relations. These skills are beneficial in day-to-day business communication."

Bill listened closely. He was confident he had dropped the ball on this and was paying for it now.

As they wound up their video call, at Raj's behest, Bill committed to finding a media coach and getting a few sessions in right away. His life wasn't getting any easier.

Avoiding the media on the tailings spill hadn't worked out as his communications manager and lawyer suggested. Pressure was mounting. The latest development was what he learned from their operations people in Nevada. It seemed the local Fire Chief wasn't happy with Bill and the company and about the lack of information flowing to the community. Residents were talking about how the company had decided not to sponsor the annual Sustainability Awards like they used to. They were blaming Bill as the new boss. This was all very bad timing. He couldn't afford to lose the locals' support on top of everything else.

The Hard Truth on Soft Skills

Bill learned a valuable lesson the hard way. The little things matter in reputation management. In fact, the little things often say the most about a person. Bill was unprepared and didn't value the so-called soft skills associated with communicating. Bill had those skills. After all, that's one of the reasons how he got to be CEO. He just wasn't valuing those skills when he needed them the most.

Here's a real life story about the little things that matter.

The Story of Diane: Little Things Matter

Diane was a client. She was smart, she became the President of a university … and it was controversial. She was an outsider to the community, and some internal leaders who were genuinely well qualified had been passed over for the job. That's not a welcoming environment to start with, but it got worse.

A disgruntled employee leaked Diane's salary, along with her generous benefit package. The grumbling started internally and transitioned to local media. It was a less than ideal situation, especially when a big part of Diane's job was improving the culture.

Imagine being Diane. It feels like the entire world is out to get you. Forget about boardroom politics … Diane had to survive politics out in the parking lot! It was a hostile environment, and she knew full well it was only going to get worse. Diane had taken a quick look at the books when she took over. She knew an inevitable storm was on the horizon. Layoffs were coming.

We had no control over the compensation package. We had to look at anything we had control over. As we poured over the compensation package, we noticed the President's parking spot. It was away from the main parking lot and right next to a side door close to the office. The President could come to work every day and, in theory, wouldn't have to see any employees. That side door was looking more attractive to Diane by the minute, but it was also a potential win in other ways.

We made a suggestion to Diane and, to her credit, she jumped on it. She gave up that spot and made it available for VIP visits. She chose to park out front, like everyone else, walk in the front door, stand in line in the cafe and have conversations with frontline workers.

On paper, this is not a big deal. Yet, very quickly we noticed the benefits. The President was being seen daily. She was having conversations with staff and seeing how morale was going. Most importantly, it humanized her at a very challenging time. The senior team appreciated the consideration and word quickly spread.

Don't dismiss the little things. They speak volumes.

Postscript: Diane is still President. Grumbling about her salary has largely disappeared. Layoffs have come and gone. Two years later, the university is profitable, while employee morale is at an all time high.

The Story of Amanda: Keep Your Enemies Close

Amanda was in charge of a large industrial foundry operation facing a huge environmental challenge: emissions were too high and needed to be cleaned up. Like many cleanup operations, this would require a significant financial investment. That was money spent on equipment, not salaries to unionized employees. It was not public yet, but was going to be soon.

Before the news got out, we advised Amanda to come up with a list of who was going to potentially have something to say about the project. The goals were twofold: (a) brief them on what was happening, but, more importantly, (b) ask them for their advice on how to best communicate it.

We were looking for common ground to build some cooperation. We were intentionally asking our future opponents to become part of the solution instead of the problem.

Amanda's first meeting was with the union leaders. Their main concern was the capital expenditure and the potential impact on job security. We reassured them that jobs were safe. In fact, the project would help with long-term sustainability and, therefore, the health and safety of the workers. With that, the union President opened up and even offered his public endorsement for the project.

Amanda worked very hard to develop a "unity message" (i.e. "We all want the same thing, which is for the company to be profitable, sustainable, and employing as many people as possible"). We told the union we would love to hire more people because that would mean we are more profitable. It was a message that resonated because it was rooted in the absolute truth.

The very concept of meeting with the union about a large capital expenditure that wasn't to do with salaries was a new way of doing things. There was no obligation to meet with them, but it paid dividends.

Bring Adversaries on Board

On the same project, we met with environmental groups and talked about what was going to happen and why it was a good thing. We knew there would be cynicism surrounding *why* the changes were happening—it wasn't happening voluntarily. Amanda was open and honest: It was happening because of changes in the government regulator's requirements, not out of the goodness of the company's heart. We addressed it rather than fudged it. We didn't treat the environmental groups like they were stupid, and they appreciated the grown-up conversation.

Finally, Amanda met with local residents in a Town Hall format. The focus was on openness and transparency, with all of her department leaders in attendance to take questions for over three hours. The leaders were given communications coaching ahead of time, so they felt comfortable knowing the main message, how to deal with challenging questions, and how to push certain questions to the senior leaders with more experience in these areas.

Gather Third-Party Endorsements

In the end, the news release announcing the project had quotes and endorsements from the union, the residents, and the environmental group. Those third-party endorsements are a huge win when communicating something that could have easily gone the wrong way.

Amanda's story went from:
Local Employer Threatens Jobs by Reluctantly Investing in New Technology
to
Local Company Embraces Opportunity to Have Cleaner Air and a Healthier Community.

It was a challenging situation that she leveraged into an opportunity.

What Connections Do You Need to Make?

The fact is companies and people mess up. So do CEOs. Often it's unintentional, while other times it is a matter of poor judgment. Either way, sooner or later, if you're running a company, something is going to happen. The question becomes *when* that happens will you have the goodwill of third party groups? Will you have relationships within media that will, at minimum, give you the benefit of the doubt on subjective aspects of the controversial issue? Will *you* survive? It all adds up in forming public opinion.

Now you may be saying to yourself, "I don't care about public opinion; it has no impact on my business." We'd reply with: "Do you have shareholders? Are you regulated in any way by government agencies? Can politicians who influence government agencies and things like taxation, zoning and enforcement make your life difficult in any way?"

If the answer is yes to any of those questions, we have news for you: Politicians, and even major shareholders with a public image, answer to regular people who spend hours on social media, and read, watch and listen to the news. If you're in the commercial sector—if you sell products to people—appreciate that people are fickle and can shift loyalties on a dime. Crisis can be a lonely place.

Earned Media and the Reputational Bank Account

Even if in many cases you can't anticipate a crisis or un-ring a bell that's been rung, you can put in the heavy lifting during "peacetime" to build some capacity and secure goodwill for future use. Think of it like a reputational bank account. You can make deposit after deposit of good news. Then, one rainy day, you're going to need to make a huge withdrawal from that reputational bank account to save your ass. At that point, the account empties, and you'll need to fill it up again.

In that regard, positive "earned media" associated with community projects and sponsorships is a gift that keeps on giving. That newspaper story, radio interview or television panel you were featured in will be shared by the media outlets to their huge social media audiences. Other interested people will then share it further to their networks. Earned media, therefore, increases your third-party credibility—in some cases reaching more people than the original news story. This rarely happens with ads or paid media.

If you weren't already convinced, consider this: earned media boosts online traffic. It can have a positive impact on organic SEO (search engine optimization) for your website or brand—something paid media can't do.

Having your company in the news in a positive way also helps attract new talent—a major challenge in a number of sectors. Recruiting is competitive, yet most potential recruits will begin their research on Google. They will search your institution, and you personally, to see what's being said in the public domain. They will try to get a flavor for who you are and why you do what you do. If you are getting a lot of positive earned media, that will show up high on your Google search results. The potential recruit reads those news stories and judges if you and your company are worth consideration. If you're looking to recruit top talent, they will have options, but the public perception of the company can be a differentiating factor in that decision-making.

What We Learned from the "Christmas Miracle"

There are some great examples of companies doing it right. They are filling that reputational bank account through earned media and marketing.

In Canada, there's a small/mid-sized airline named WestJet. Often described as the Southwest Airlines of Canada, the company had already developed a bit of a viral following because of the friendly nature of many of their flight attendants. Then Christmas 2013 happened.

As we all know, airports are extremely stressful during the holiday season. Bad weather and cancelled flights combined with the longest lines of the year and stressed-out travelers trying to get somewhere is a deadly PR cocktail for any airline.

WestJet managed to find out what their passengers at the Toronto and Hamilton airports had on their Christmas wish lists. When those people boarded, more than 150 WestJet employees went to work. They had about three hours before the planes would land in Calgary. They gathered the presents, got them wrapped and delivered to the airport in Calgary as the passengers were landing. Those passengers were shocked, and the entire process from beginning to end was captured on hidden cameras.

The video is incredibly compelling. WestJet said it would donate flights to needy families if the video got at least 200,000 views on YouTube. At the time of this writing, it had received almost 50 million. WestJet filled that reputational bank account all the way to the top.

The proof is clear. WestJet is far from perfect. It's an airline, after all. It cancels people's important flights. It loses their luggage. It misleads customers. At one point, it even had five bomb threats in one week. However, it didn't keep customers away. Most people trust WestJet, warts and all.

This is a heightened example, but you get the point. More than ever, it is vital to be proactive in ensuring your company engages with its communities. People have so many avenues to communicate and share bad experiences, so build relationships with key stakeholders. Work hard at telling positive stories and making an impact in the communities where you operate.

People expect more today. They expect social responsibility, and they expect some semblance of transparency and connection. They are empowered to speak out when they aren't happy. Otherwise, sit back and wait at your own peril. You may not think of this as crisis communications; however, these are all tools in the preparation toolbox. If a crisis happens and your company already has a challenged reputation, don't go looking for goodwill because you won't find it.

Developing goodwill and relationships is within your power—you have full control over it. The only thing stopping you from maximizing goodwill is you.

3 Steps to Peace-Time Public Relations

When a crisis hits it is too late to start building key relationships that may be able to help you through a tough situation or through a "war." You are short on time. Action is what is required and speed is essential.

Here are a few simple approaches to developing key, meaningful relationships when times are good and calm; relationships that could help or hinder you when war breaks out:

1. **Media:** Identify key local, national and "beat" journalists (bloggers). Reach out and schedule breakfast with them (nothing fancy ... and do breakfast because most reporters are so busy they don't have time for a meaningful lunch break). You are not there to solicit them to do a story on your company; that's what they will expect, so surprise them. The purpose is to get to know them (they should be talking more than you). You want to ask them questions about their needs, their deadlines, advice they may have for you and your team. Invite them to come see your operations some time. Offer to pick up the tab, but don't be surprised if they insist on covering their own bill as a symbolic way of communicating their neutrality. Follow up with a thank-you email. Give them your personal number if they ever need anything. In the future, if you have a good, positive story,

consider leaking it to one of the identified main media influencers. Journalists love scoops.

2. **Special Interest Groups:** Identify groups that do, or may in the future, oppose your company or your sector. So, for example, if you're a mining company that could be an environmental group. Follow the same procedures as point 1 above. Meet them. Get to know them and what makes them tick. It doesn't mean they'll suddenly support you, but it could mean that in a crisis situation they'll at least be willing to hear you out on what happened before going nuts on you in the national media.

3. **Politicians:** In keeping with the outreach theme, identify the federal, state/provincial and municipal/regional elected officials that represent both the geographical areas where you operate and the ones who have oversight or critical roles for your sector. Politicians are generalists, but they are generalists who have huge voices with the media. Your role in getting to know them is to educate them on what you and your company are all about, how you are helping their constituents, and to open a direct line of communication. Foster that relationship over time because not only do politicians have direct media inputs, they also have governance roles with your regulators.

Are You Playing the Long Game?

The strategy Raj was following was a longer-term play. The company would develop meaningful connections and get to know the journalists and stakeholders a bit better. Essentially, you're meeting with two key groups of people:

   a) People who can make your situation exponentially better when an issue or crisis happens; and

b) People who can make your life considerably worse when an issue or crisis happens.

Journalists fall into both categories, so it can't hurt you to develop relationships when you don't want anything from them, educating them about what you do and why you're doing it, and letting them know you are a helpful resource to them on any related issue in the future. It helps build capacity for the future.

The same capacity-building needs to take place with groups that can help or hinder you when you stumble. Consider if you were a journalist, who would you call for comment for your story? In the case of Raj, that would be groups he met with, like Mental Health America, the National Alliance on Mental Health, the American Psychiatric Association, and the American Mental Health Counselors Association. These are all groups the media would call if Shlomo became a news story, so why not get to know them when times are good? Your worst-case scenario is they learn about what you do and become advocates and ambassadors for what you do, knowing that online counseling is like a gateway that leads to sitting down with a face-to-face professional in many situations. It may come off as sales, but what you're doing is building credibility and informing the very people reporters will want to speak to when an issue comes up.

On this tour, the organizations and media would focus on understanding what it is they need from someone like Raj, his company and his leaders. Raj was going to be asking a lot of questions about what they do, what they need and what they think. These meetings would have room to breathe and evolve. It was a soft sell, if any sell at all.

How much are you like Bill? Are you great at what you do, but not necessarily aware of the broader reputational picture? There's a good chance you are reading this contrast with Raj and noticing you are more like Bill than you care to admit. If it is any consolation, it puts you in the majority.

Most corporate leaders don't invest much time nor energy in what many of them call "soft skills," like relationship-building outside the obvious stakeholders in their business world. However, the good ones do and that is what you will consider moving forward because it could save your reputation one day.

When it comes to stakeholders beyond the media, ask yourself which organizations and special interest groups could either make your life Hell or Heaven in a reputational crisis?

Takeaways

- Get media coaching when times are calm. Build capacity.
- Fill the reputational bank account for a withdrawal later.
- Look for the common ground with potential opponents early on.

Questions to Ask Yourself: When a crisis happens, who will be in your war room and what will their roles be? Who is your crisis communications team and how will you gather them quickly?

CHAPTER 5

Check Yourself before You Wreck Yourself

Four Days Later

Bill was feeling emboldened. He had taken Raj's advice and found someone who could give his team a media training session. But Bill was also feeling frustrated. The tailings spill was still an issue for public debate. It was time to put this thing to bed. He was done talking about it.

He had gathered his senior leadership team to put an end to the dithering. Sitting down at the table, he opened the conversation with a directive: "I don't want to hear about why we shouldn't talk about this anymore. I want to know how to end the conversation."

That kicked off a robust debate. Some members of the team, such as his legal counsel, argued that ignoring the issue would cause it to wither and die. Others argued in favour of getting out in front of the problem and cutting it off. One person suggested Bill himself go and meet a couple of the main journalists, but to do it in an "off the record" capacity. This last suggestion gave Bill reason to pause, but his instincts said no. It was too late for that now. The gate was open and the horse had bolted.

It was his Director of Investor Relations who first floated the idea of addressing the issue head-on, better late than never. "Look, Bill," he said, "We do earnings calls with our investors and we do them via conference call, right? We do that to get it done and over with. Let's do that with the media. Let's take them all on at once, and get this over and done with, fully on the record."

That evening, Nicholas, the Board Chair, found Bill in his office. Everyone else had gone home. It was dark with only a desk lamp illuminating the office. Nick interrupted the silence with, "I thought I'd stick around and help you prepare for tomorrow's news conference."

Bill felt bad. This was taking up far too much time. Isn't that why he had taken that media training course a few weeks ago? "I appreciate the sentiment, Nick, but I'm okay. We had some media training. Go home and get some rest."

Nicholas shrugged. He wasn't going to force him to practice.

The next day, Bill was standing on the bank of the reconstructed tailings pond. Facing him were media from a half dozen news outlets.

It started well. Bill was able to answer all the questions in a way he had rehearsed. He was calm, confident and caring. He pointed to all the hard work the company had done to repair the tailings pond. He was confident the problem wouldn't be repeated.

That was when one reporter asked an innocent question: "How do you know?"

"Excuse me?" asked Bill.

"I mean, how do you know that the tailings pond won't leak again? Are you personally going to guarantee it?"

"Well, okay, that's a fair point," admitted Bill. "I guess what's fair to say is that—"

"So, you don't know that it won't happen again," interrupted another reporter.

"Hey, as I was just explaining, this incident was an exceptional event. We have built this wall to new standards, and—"

"New standards? So, the old wall wasn't up to code?" asked a third reporter.

"Well, that's not accurate. The new wall goes above and beyond, while we examine what happened in the past—"

That opened up a floodgate of questions.

"Can we look at the maintenance records?"

"Is it true it wasn't maintained properly?"

"Are the new standards going to prevent this from happening?"

"Who was responsible for maintenance on the old wall?"

Bill quieted the throng: "I get it. You have a lot of questions. Right now I'm still trying to get answers. I get it. I want answers too! I can promise you that we're doing everything we can to look at what happened. We're doing everything we can to prevent it from failing again."

Another reporter chimed in. "Has anyone been disciplined as part of this process?"

Bill saw an opportunity and took it. "We have suspended the engineer and the maintenance crew. They were responsible for maintaining the retaining wall. We want to take a close look at exactly what happened, and make sure it doesn't happen again."

The reporter closed his notebook and sat back. Other reporters asked some routine follow-up questions, and the news conference dispersed.

The following morning, Bill was awoken by a phone call from the Board Chair. Nick was furious. "What have you done?" he barked. "Look at the newspaper."

Bill stumbled over to his laptop and pulled up the website. That's where he saw a story that made his stomach twist into a solid knot.

The headline was large, clear, and damning: UNION CLAIMS SAFETY COMPROMISED: MINING BOSS ADMITS HE HAS NO ANSWERS.

There were several pictures accompanying the story. One was Bill, standing on top of his freshly repaired wall. Beside that photo was a picture of a dead bird, decomposing on the shores of a body of water. The newspaper claimed the photo was taken only 300 feet from where the news conference was held. The third photo was of the National Union President and he was angry.

The story went on to claim Bill was in a last-ditch effort to save his own skin. Suspending the workers was a pathetic attempt to find a scapegoat and the Union wouldn't stand for it.

The Union claimed Bill was responsible for short-staffing the mine. There used to be 200 dedicated maintenance crew on site, the union man stated. Now there were 124 staff and it was obvious that safety was taking a back seat to profits. It was clear the newspaper wasn't going to take Bill's word for it.

He was kicking himself. Why hadn't he sent out a team to clean up the site before the reporters arrived?

Nevertheless, the Union accusations weren't accurate. There were maybe 124 dedicated maintenance crew, but there were still 200 people in total. Some had been reassigned to roles to make the site more efficient. The employees were happier for the most part. It was a visionary plan and it had nothing to do with maintenance at the retaining pond. The Union didn't like it because they felt the company was positioning itself for future layoffs.

Bill was furious. This article wasn't going to stop the questions. This made things worse. Now he wasn't just "hiding." He was incompetent.

How did he go from calm and in control to a bumbling corporate stooge?

Facts vs. Feelings

Bill made two of the easiest mistakes you can make when it comes to a corporate crisis. The first was that it's not just about facts; it's about feelings.

Bill relied on the facts exclusively. While facts are foundationally crucial in working a crisis, you need more than just facts to get through one successfully. Perception is reality and perception is formed by not only facts, but by emotional content.

Emotions are what drive stories. Emotions are what create reactions. Emotions are what people respond to. The facts merely act as a framework to hold all that emotional energy in one place. **Facts tell, but stories sell.** And stories are driven by emotion.

You see, it's only a crisis if people are upset with you. If a grandfather dies inside your sports venue, do you have a crisis? Again, it depends. If a grandfather dies in a hospital, that's a family tragedy, but it's not necessarily a crisis. What's the difference? The difference is people expect older folks to die in a hospital. So, the issue lies not in the fact that grandpa died; it lies in the fact that people are *upset* about grandpa dying.

Now when the public get it in their head that you're somehow responsible for grandpa dying, that's when you start to have a bad day from a communications perspective. Obviously, grandpa dying in an arena may not be a relevant example for you, but the point we're hoping you carry away here is that you will not get into a crisis because of anything that happens. You will get into a crisis based on how people feel about what happened.

The Story of a Guitar, an Airline … and a Media Scandal

Take the story of Dave Carroll. Dave is a professional musician from Nova Scotia, Canada.

Dave is the classic everyman. His whole schtick is to be relatable, and he wears plaid instead of suits and ties. He and his brother run the band "Sons of Maxwell." Why that name? Their father's name is Maxwell. Dave is not a complicated man.

Dave was sitting on a United Airlines jet awaiting a flight from Chicago to Nebraska. That's when he saw baggage handlers carelessly toss his Taylor guitar case. Sure enough, when he landed he confirmed the worst: his guitar was broken. But that's only the beginning of the drama.

Dave could tell you about the weeks of back-and-forth phone calls … calls spent attempting to get United to do the right thing and pay for the repairs to his guitar. He could tell you about the bad attitude or the rejection he got when he tried to file a claim.

But he won't tell you about that. He did something even more damaging than simply tell it to you.

See, Dave is a musician. And after being rejected for the umpteenth time by bureaucrats at United Airlines, Dave issued a simple threat. "If I were a lawyer, I'd sue you. But I'm not a lawyer; I'm a singer/songwriter. So, I'm going to write a song about you instead."

United Airlines would grow to rue their decision to ignore Dave.

Dave wrote a catchy tune and created his own music video. The song was called, aptly enough, "United Breaks Guitars." The song did something no other piece of content had ever managed to do up to that point—go viral. It was one of the very first viral videos in YouTube history.

Within days, "United Breaks Guitars" was the talk of the aviation industry. It was being discussed by all the major television networks. It was funny. It was catchy. It made United Airlines look horrible. The song told the story. It was the medium that delivered.

UBG came out around the same time as some unrelated bad news for United. It all led to a significant decline in shareholder value. And when United lost close to $1 billion in stock value within a week, the media were quick to point out why. It was obvious: it was because they break guitars.

The backlash was severe. United Airlines replaced Dave Carroll's guitar.

(Postscript: approximately a year later, they lost Dave's luggage again. That was enough to make headlines, again. If we were United, we would treat Dave's luggage with more attention than the nuclear launch codes.)

The whole nasty, ugly situation could have been completely avoided. United wouldn't be the laughing stock of an entire industry. They wouldn't be the butt of parody songs on YouTube or late-night jokes on TV. But they also committed the second mistake ... they let their ego get in the way.

In our story, Bill is in trouble, because he's also committing the second mistake: his ego is blinding him.

When Emotions or Ego Override Common Sense

Don't set yourself up to be a villain for the sake of your own ego or emotions. When you become the villain for the sake of your own emotions, you're setting yourself up to lose.

After all, Dave Carroll didn't get 15 million hits on YouTube because United broke his guitar. He didn't find a lucrative public speaking career because United broke his guitar. He found his fame and fortune because United allowed emotions to own the narrative.

Dave got mad, he got emotional, and he found a powerful way to communicate emotion in a way that connected with people because most of us know what it's like to have our luggage damaged or go missing.

Voila! United loses a billion bucks, Dave gets a new guitar, *and* he gets a lucrative career.

The CEO with an Uber Ego

It's not only Dave Carroll fighting over a broken guitar. Look at Uber. Travis Kalanick, the former CEO, is a poster child of someone who appears to have let his ego get in the way of smart thinking.

Kalanick was the Golden Boy to Silicon Valley investors. Uber started as a mere idea and within only a few years it was the most valuable transportation company on earth. But simply because Uber matured, Kalanick didn't at the same pace. He got into some hot water and took Uber on a ride with him.

Uber had an aggressive expansion policy. It didn't matter if a city council welcomed Uber; if Uber wanted into your city, they were coming. It was part of their modus operandi. This policy tended to create lots of media attention. Most of it was negative.

That aggressive approach is manageable if it's handled well. Kalanick could have adopted a "Well, it's unfortunate we were forced into doing it this way" approach. If he could be calm and reasoned, he would have been fine. People may not have liked it but they would have understood it. They may have fought him on it but at a core level they would have accepted his approach. Kalanick would have been more trusted (and Uber along with him).

The sad thing about this is that Uber is built on trust. Uber smartly and simply addresses all the problems with the traditional taxi industry. It kicks that old-school industry right in the face.

- Don't like smelly, rude drivers? Rate your driver.
- Don't like high fares? We'll keep it reasonable.
- Don't like going the long way around in a strange city? Watch exactly where you're going on the app.
- Don't like hearing a cab is on the way and then waiting 30 minutes? Watch your car come straight to you on the app.
- Don't like having to produce the exact change, or cabbies who bitch about you paying with Visa? Heck, you don't even need to get out your wallet.

In a lot of ways, the app is brilliant. But Kalanick was taken out behind the woodshed and shot by his Board of Directors.

Rather than presenting a calm, mild-mannered approach when confronted by upset cities, Kalanick doubled down. In fact, Uber declared war. It came to a head in 2014, when Uber had to apologize for hiring investigators to dig up dirt on journalists.

That was only the beginning. Controversy after controversy followed. Kalanick was accused of fostering a "bro culture" which wasn't helped when he told a reporter the company was referred internally to as "Boober."

Ultimately, the Board had enough and forced Kalanick to resign in June of 2017. Kalanick could have been the CEO of the largest transportation company on earth. He's not, arguably because he let his ego dictate his decision-making.

But sadly, stupid controversies driven by ego aren't exclusive to Uber.

Choose Your Words Wisely

While we're beating up on United Airlines, we can mention them one last time. You would think they learned a lesson from broken guitars, but no. In 2017, Dr. David Dao was beaten and removed from a United flight after he refused to give up his seat.

Did United have a right to demand his seat? According to the Conditions of Carriage—the fine print on a ticket—yes. Should they have taken his seat? That's arguable. Did they do it the right way? No.

They let emotions get in the way. When Dao refused to accommodate their demand, he was bloodied and beaten. Consequently, so was United Airlines.

Famous Last Words: "72 ... 92 ... whatever"

Perhaps the pinnacle of ego overriding brains came in 1995, with the Chair and CEO of Dow Corning, Richard Hazleton.

Dow Corning was embroiled in the silicon breast implant scandal. Women were complaining that their breast implants were making them sick. It was becoming a huge problem for Dow Corning and they were embroiled in a fight with lawyers, US Food and Drug Administration regulators and alleged victims.

Dow, of course, was vehemently protesting its innocence. In their minds, the facts didn't back up the claims the women's health activists were making. Hazleton thought he could handle the heat and did the ultimate high-risk, high-reward media play we've ever seen ... he agreed to appear on *Oprah*.

Keep in mind, the optics of this are horrible. This is a middle-aged male CEO talking about a women's health issue (and because we're talking about larger breasts, arguably a misogynistic women's health issue) on the most popular female-oriented television show on the planet.

Things were going okay for Hazleton. Not horrible, but he was holding his own until about 44 minutes into the hour-long show. A member of the audience appeared on camera and spent two solid minutes ripping Hazleton to shreds, and accused him of promoting junk science. A dispute arose over the number of deaths.

At one point, Hazleton began to speak about 92 deaths. The activist interrupted to point out the number was 72 (which, technically, is in Hazleton's favor). Hazleton's response? "72, 92 … whatever."

It was a momentary slip but one he didn't come back from. Hazleton became so fixated on proving his attackers wrong and proving why he was right he lost sight of the bigger picture. He needed to provide a human face to Dow Corning. He did, but that human face was a sanctimonious male know-it-all.

Just three syllables, "Whatever." That "Whatever" arguably helped cost him over three-billion dollars in class action settlements.

Common Communications Traps for Executives

Most leaders are good people. But sadly, we've seen it time and time again.

Corporate leaders continue to drive decisions from their ego and as a result they don't just fall into trouble—they dive into it. Here are some of the most common mistakes corporate leaders make. Have you been guilty of any of the following?

1. Believing your existing team is up to the challenge of handling a crisis.

This is a brutal mistake and it's entirely understandable. Overestimating a team's abilities happens for two reasons.

The first reason is that the leader doesn't know what to look for. When you don't know what to look for, it's easy to not get the skills you need. It's not malicious; it's an overconfidence of ability. All communications professionals think they can do their job well. And, while many are excellent at corporate communications, crisis management is a highly specialized field.

Ninety percent of North American drivers consider themselves "better than average" drivers. Think about that. It's mathematically impossible. Professional communicators are no different.

If your Director of Communications has never worked in the media at a high-pressure level, they won't know what it's like in a corporate newsroom. They're not lying to you about experience ... they *think* they know. They can't know what they don't know.

The second reason a team's abilities are overestimated is because the team itself will tell you the team is good enough. We hear expressions like, "Oh, we've got a team with crisis communications experience." But if your team dealt with a small crisis three years ago, does that make them experienced? Does an occasional recall qualify them to be crisis veterans?

Having someone who occasionally dabbles in crisis is the same thing as a weekend warrior who straps on boxing gloves. If you spar in a workout session once a week, does that make you a good fighter? Put that same fighter up against someone who bare-knuckle boxes every single day ... and *likes* it. That's not even fair.

You tell us who's going to emerge the victor.

2. Overestimating your own crisis communications abilities.

Smart leaders know they don't know it all. That's why they surround themselves with the best people. Overestimating your ability to handle a high-stakes situation is toxic. That's called gambling with your own chips. Bill assumed a single day of media coaching would prepare him for a news conference. He was mistaken and he paid for it with his reputation. What caused it? It was his ego, pure and simple.

We see it in corporate boardrooms across the globe. We see it with the leader who cracks a joke because they didn't read the room. Or the leader who gets so used to handling routine media queries that she doesn't sweat during a crisis moment. A little bit of nervousness is a good thing—it reminds you how serious this is and the consequences of what you're doing.

You may not be glib enough to call your company "Boober," but we see corporate leaders shrug off critical moments day after day and they get away with it … until they don't.

3. Believing you can never be replaced.

Wayne Gretzky won four Stanley Cups in four years. He not only broke multiple NHL records; he shattered them. As hockey fans will know, Wayne Gretzky was traded away at the age of 27 at the height of his career.

We have seen C-Suite leaders with an exaggerated sense of personal loyalty. We have seen a Board of Directors fire those leaders at a moment's notice to protect the company. The leaders who get into trouble tend to overlook this simple fact: the team around them doesn't care about the CEO.

The lawyer who's giving legal advice to the CEO? He's not specifically concerned about the CEO. He works for the company, not the CEO. It's a simple truth, but it's easy to forget.

Any Board of Directors, when given a choice between the reputation of their CEO and the reputation of their company, will pick the company. Every single time.

4. Not encouraging a "Truth to Power" environment.

Ego is almost a healthy requirement with CEOs. Smart leaders recognize this and take steps to encourage constructive dissent. There's nothing shameful in being wrong. What's damaging is when the leader wants an honest opinion or insight and can't find it.

Smart leaders have a secret. The only way to understand what's going on is to find a source that will tell them directly.

Find a trusted source. Find several. We see this throughout the book when Raj talks to Carrie in a trusted relationship. Carrie is free to speak the truth to Raj. Sometimes, even though they mean well, the "yes men" around Raj are afraid to speak up.

5. Catering to social media opinion.

There is a difference between showing leadership and catering to the masses. You likely already know this, otherwise you wouldn't be a leader. Some leaders confuse genuine public opinion with social media slacktivism.

Social media channels can be loud and are important to monitor in crisis communications situations because the mainstream media monitors trends for story angles. Unfortunately, those same social media channels are dominated by "social justice warriors" who jump on the issue of the day and share their opinion, educated or not.

Be cautious making fundamental strategic and tactical decisions based on what people are saying on Twitter, Reddit or Facebook.

Should You Ever Talk Off the Record?

You can technically agree with a reporter that you're off the record but, in reality, don't share anything you don't want to appear in a news story with your name attached to it.

Why? Well, because even the media can't agree on what "off the record" means. Are you sure you want to put your trust in that process?

The fact is that even in journalism circles there is no hard and fast rule clearly stating the meaning of "off the record." Most of the major media outlets have differing interpretations of what it means. Even journalism legend Bob Woodward (played by Robert Redford in *All the President's Men*) is clear that "off the record" doesn't mean you're safe, as he told the Poynter Institute back in 2011:

> *"If somebody tells you something is off the record, some people think that you can lock it in a box by saying 'off the record' and it will never appear in print. If that were the case, you'd have people like Nixon saying, 'Off the record, I did it all,' and then you could never use it. It would be absurd."*

Here's another iconic journalist, Seymour Hersh, back in 1976:

> *"Theoretically, off the record means you can't use it. Most people think off the record means you can use it but there can't be any connection whatsoever to them. During Watergate I had one lawyer say, "off-off-off the record," and I wasn't sure I wanted to hear it. You have a real problem whether to use it. Most of the time you try to clarify. It's different with everyone. It's complicated."*

It's complicated. Exactly. With the evolution of social media "off the record" has become way more complicated then when Seymour Hersh spoke about it in 1976.

If it is vital the information be reported for whatever reason—but it can't in any way be connected to you—there are other methods of getting that information to the reporter that don't involve your name. Consult an expert. Protect your name.

Where Did Bill Go Wrong?

In our story, Bill got into trouble because he felt practicing his forthcoming media appearance was beneath him. He justified it by saying that practice meant taking up the time of the Board Chair.

Bill clearly felt he knew what he was doing. After all, he had taken a media training course. His pride told him that practice would be a waste of time. Bill's pride orchestrated his fall. He let his ego get in the way.

Takeaways

- Never let ego get in the way of smart decision-making.
- Managing a crisis isn't just about facts; emotions are crucial.
- Assuming your existing team can handle a crisis isn't a failure on their part—it's a failure of your ego overriding smart decision-making.

Question to Ask Yourself: Do you have public/media holding-statement templates ready for any potential crisis situation?

CHAPTER 6

The Danger of DIY Crisis Communications

Ten Days Later

Bill was at home with a coffee. He was exhausted. His wife was at work and the kids were at school. He sat waiting but there was no video call from Raj. He was twenty minutes late and that never happens. Bill wasn't complaining though—he was enjoying the few moments of peace and quiet.

His life had been utter chaos with ongoing media calls. Somehow they had found his home number and were calling there now. The coverage had gone national and his kids were even hearing it at school from some of the teachers.

Bill wasn't sleeping or eating. The stress was mounting and he knew his job could be on the line. The public was calling for a pound of flesh.

He had started working from home because it was hard to get anything done at the office. Going to the community near the mine site was out of the question with the hostility there lately. Bill had been there the week earlier to make a presentation to the local government council and it didn't go well.

His communications manager had prepared a presentation for Bill to give. It was light on details and heavy on pandering rhetoric. At one point, a local councillor made some very critical comments about the presentation. Bill responded with some poor body language when he rolled his eyes and shrugged. The councillor lost his cool, with the state media reporting the entire thing. Bill was becoming a liability and now the politicians were getting unsettled with the company's response. It was bad.

There comes a time during every crisis when a leader takes stock of what has happened, what is happening and what may be coming down the line. He or she determines if they have control of the situation and if not, why not. For Bill, that realization was happening now. His conclusion was that he depended too heavily on his in-house staff, when what he needed were specialists. He owned his part in this debacle and that included not bringing in the right people. Bill needed to put out the fire fast.

He picked up the crisis communications plan they paid for, the one Bill never actually read from beginning to end. He didn't have time to get through that much material. Regardless, the Board said it simply needed to "check a box." An expensive box. Bill called the number on the back page—the contact for the communications "guru" who did all the TED talks and corporate speaking engagements.

He had searched her name online when they first engaged her and she certainly seemed legitimate. She was well-spoken and light on her feet as she paced back and forth on the stage with a headset microphone. She turned every so often to acknowledge a slick or funny graphic on the massive monitor behind her. The crowd loved her. She had authored a number of books and done countless media interviews. Bill needed her now more than ever and price wasn't even a consideration at this point.

"I'm sorry. I don't actually work crisis situations," the voice said on the other end of the line.

Know What to Look For

Bill didn't know what he wanted in a crisis communications specialist. Neither did his Board. He was drowning and needed a life preserver. So, he did what most people do in situations like this. He pulled out his smartphone and searched "crisis communications companies near me" on the internet.

There certainly was no shortage of options in the Denver area. Bill picked up the phone and called a huge agency with offices across the United States. They did everything. Marketing. Videos. Websites. Media strategy. Political campaigns. Coaching. Speech writing. You name it, they did it. Although their staff biographies didn't list anyone with a media background, they also listed crisis communications.

Bill got a VP on the line and that VP knew exactly who Bill and his company were and the crisis they had been going through. They got on it immediately with a minimum starting retainer of $200,000. Unfortunately, some agencies can smell desperation. They know companies and executives will pay whatever they have to in order to save themselves.

Bill told the VP that his company had a crisis communications plan and he'd send it over right away. However, the VP told him to keep it. His agency couldn't depend on the research or analysis of another company purely for liability and best-practice purposes. Bill didn't have much in the way of choices at this point, so he gave the new agency the green light and had procurement issue the sole-source approval and cut the check.

Don't Be the Scapegoat

The "rapid response" was slower than Bill expected. Pressure was mounting and their new crisis communications company spent over a week getting up to speed. Later in the week, an email came in and he knew what it was the minute he saw it …

Meantime, 1500 miles away in Boston, Raj had his own crisis brewing. He was standing in his company's lobby with the police following a break-in at the head office of Shlomo. Thieves had gotten away with all the computers. But that wasn't what had Raj concerned.

His IT guys told him a few of the laptops taken hadn't been encrypted yet. They were full of private health information of customers. This was going to be a huge problem.

Raj excused himself for a moment and took out his mobile phone. "Hi, Carrie. It's Raj down at Shlomo. We need your crisis team."

Trust Experience

Using only in-house resources is what we call DIY crisis communications: do-it-yourself. However, unlike DIY kitchen renovation and DIY landscaping, DIY crisis communications can be fatal from a reputational perspective.

Would you do DIY heart surgery? DIY gas line repair? No. However, everyone thinks they're a communications expert. They don't realize how much experience is required to navigate through it properly until it's too late.

Experienced crisis communicators are the ones smart people call when all Hell is breaking loose and they need experienced navigators to get them out alive. What experienced crisis communicators have, they can't fully teach. It's experience-based. Even this book is intended to give you high-level perspective on broad approaches to crisis management.

We've been in rooms with executives responding emotionally in the face of great personal and corporate adversity. They thought they had a plan and now it was up to these outsiders with experience in the ring to get them through it. You see, everyone has a plan until they get punched in the face, as boxing legend Mike Tyson once said.

What Not to Say When You're Punched in the Face

Nowhere is this advice more relevant than in the corporate world where the punch is a reputational attack that can end your career. The world is full of people who had it all until they said the wrong thing to the media. If you think you're above that or immune to that, then you haven't been punched yet.

The Story of Larry: Find Your Softer Side

Have you ever picked up a newspaper and read about some developer trying to build condos, only to face huge public opposition at an open-house meeting? Usually what happens next is that politicians get involved "on behalf of the people." It happens all the time ... and in most cases, a crisis is completely preventable.

Larry was a property developer, and a client of ours trying to build condos on a very sensitive and picturesque piece of land. His company had spent millions on the property and now needed zoning approval. Unfortunately for Larry, a number of city councillors had already expressed their concerns about the project. We worked with Larry to develop a detailed outreach strategy that involved one-on-one meetings with every councillor. But he knew that one-on-one meetings alone weren't going to do it for him.

Any time you discuss zoning changes, public meetings are part of that decision-making process. Those public meetings would be critical. Larry was terrified by the prospect of a community activist yelling at city councillors for the benefit of the media.

Rather than sit and merely hope, we sat down with Larry and got to work, making a few critical changes to the strategy. We focused on a very transparent and accessible open house. We had plenty of refreshments, visual boards and video renderings of what people would see.

Larry decided to sell an environmentally advanced condo building that would bring the community into the 21st century. We gave communications coaching to the entire presentation team and media coaching to the main spokesperson. Who was the main spokesperson? Not Larry.

In fact, we chose the architect as the main spokesperson. It was decided the architect could speak to "the vision." It was an artistic appeal. It was a presentation based on emotions rather than property values or land-use planning.

Larry committed some up-front resources to ensure the meetings went well—something most developers simply don't do. In the end, the meetings were stellar: Larry's proposal got excellent media coverage and the council voted unanimously in favor of the project going ahead.

Famous Last Words: "I'd Like My Life Back"

Tony Hayward, the former CEO of British Petroleum, thought he could take a punch. Boy, was he wrong. Hayward's big plan was simple: make the BP brand synonymous with safety. It was going to be his legacy at the historic company that had a history of accidents and oil spills before Hayward took over.

On April 20, 2010, Hayward got hit with a bag of bricks. He wobbled. He teetered. He tried to recover. But eventually he fell and never got up.

On that day, about 52 miles off the coast of Louisiana, in the Gulf of Mexico, BP's Deepwater Horizon oil rig suffered a catastrophic explosion. Eleven workers were killed. Millions of gallons of oil spewed into the ocean. Unto itself, a horrible tragedy.

But, as cold as this sounds, the public accepts there are risks and sometimes fatal accidents in deep sea oil drilling. From a public relations perspective, this is usually something a company and a CEO can survive. We've helped companies, executives and boards many times with multiple fatalities at play. In most situations, there is an opportunity in a crisis. There is the opportunity to convey that your openness, transparency and authenticity are traits that are present in tough times as equally as in good times.

Despite this reality, three months later, BP's CEO Tony Hayward was a loathed public personality and was fired at the height of his career. He ended up a long way from his posh digs in London and was relegated to running a much smaller company in Kurdistan. What happened to Hayward? Where did he go wrong? At the end of the day, it can be summed up as a deadly combination of ignorance and arrogance.

Glenn DaGian, a former senior communicator who left BP a year before the disaster, was interviewed by National Public Radio in the U.S. He had been brought back in to help and he stated he was very upset that the executives of the company didn't want to apologize. He said:

> "BP executives declared it was not their accident, blamed their contractors and made the company look arrogant and callous. The company's response has become a textbook example of how not to do crisis management."

DaGian wasn't surprised. He suggested that, as CEO, Hayward didn't appreciate the importance of communications and cut the budget to save money. That left Hayward, quite often, listening to rookies with very few developed platforms and external relationships to leverage. DaGian said there was no plan in place to manage this crisis or any crisis for that matter.

From a crisis communications perspective, the gaffes became too many to count after the Deep Horizon explosion/spill:

- BP wouldn't comment, allowing rumor and speculation to reign.
- BP minimized the impact of the accident in the beginning, failing to acknowledge the spill was out of control.
- BP failed to apologize early and often for what had happened.
- BP tried to blame others, including the rig operational company by saying it "was not our accident" despite being project coordinator.
- Hayward failed in conveying any sense of humanity or empathy.
- He came off as arrogant, saying BP "was up to the challenge," like it was some sort of corporate sailing competition.
- BP felt it could use marketing to get through it by running ads with Hayward saying, "We will make this right." The ads flopped horribly and were ill-advised.

However, despite all this, the real watershed moment that saw Hayward go past the reputational point of no return was on May 30, 2010. After a number of proverbial jabs, this was the haymaker punch that put him down once and for all.

After waiting way too long, Hayward and BP Oil were finally set to apologize and take some responsibility for the accident. Hayward took reporters along a beach to show them how hard they were working on the cleanup. Despite never previously accepting responsibility, he apologized for what had happened.

And, then, as if he was gagging on the words of apology, Hayward went off-script and said: "No one wants this over more than I do. I'd like my life back."

The mere suggestion that there was no one else in the world who wanted it to be over more than him was ridiculous and selfish. What about the business owners whose livelihoods were over? What about the families of the killed workers? What about local residents?

The self-centered comment was the beginning of the end for Hayward. He didn't have anyone around him who could convey the importance of saying sorry, conveying regret and validating how people felt. Those words he said were repeated over and over in the media. Even people who weren't following the story knew an arrogant CEO when they saw one and they spoke out.

It was clear he was either not getting good advice and coaching through a tough time, or that he was getting good advice and simply wasn't taking it. Either way, he was a dead CEO walking. Vegas odds makers started running bets on how long Hayward would last before being fired. The odds were reported by mainstream media.

Other CEOs survive tragic accidents with their jobs but Hayward was done. It was not because of the actual spill, not because of the environmental damage, and not because of the money it would cost to fix. Hayward was forced to resign because of the words he said and the manner in which he said them. It didn't matter that he didn't cause the oil spill … he was the scapegoat.

The Public Is Smarter Than You Think

Given the amount of information and media they consume, citizens have grown quite adept at getting their information from multiple sources. They are sharp at reading nonverbal cues like body language and tonality. They know when someone is lying or hiding something. They should be treated with respect. People have become crusaders. They have various channels to communicate to large groups and mobilize very quickly. So, as a communicator in a crisis, your only and best hope is to be transparent, honest and responsive. Deal with your truth and get ahead of it, looking for the opportunity in that crisis. As we've said before, the days of being able to "no comment" your way out of a crisis or wait it out until it goes away are long behind us.

Despite what happened to Tony Hayward and others like him, it is amazing that business leaders continue to learn these lessons over and over again.

In 2008, Maple Leaf Foods, Canadian food processing giant, got punched hard. It sold contaminated meat that ended up killing 23 people and making over 50 others very sick. Companies typically don't survive things like this. According to one business study by the Ivey School of Business, more than 5,000 media stories were written on this scandal. It was an international story.

So, why did this crisis become the case study for the right way to do it? What was their secret? Well, it wasn't anything complicated. In fact, according to the company, they kept it simple with these key tactics:

- **Act with urgency:** The CEO called a news conference the very night the outbreak began and took questions himself, sharing all of the information the company had with the public/media/customers.
- **Take accountability:** The company could have attempted to deflect the problem to a number of possible issues ranging from human error, food testing standards and equipment, but it did none of those things. It took the full blame and owned it.

- **Be transparent:** The company's internal core values stated the goals of being transparent, open and honest and they stuck with those core values throughout.

To this day, the Maple Leaf handling of this crisis is still considered the gold standard for what to do in a crisis when punched hard. So, why do most companies, CEOs and leaders not follow these gold standards when a crisis happens?

The Language of Leaders

We worked with a politician once who had a huge communications problem. No matter how much we coached, repeated and coached some more, when this person spoke publicly in the media or during a speech, the words spoken were littered with the words "I" and "me." I did this, I did that, this happened because of me, me, me.

This person simply wouldn't adjust to coaching. It turned people off. It sounds more like bragging or an inferiority complex than leadership. So, it was no surprise that person didn't last long in politics. This happens more often than you think in leadership—especially in the corporate world. Usually those leaders don't last. The funny thing is they most often don't even realize they're speaking from a self-centered perspective.

The people listening to the message—whether it's employees, shareholders, voters or stakeholders in general—may not pick up on exactly what they don't like; they only know there's a lack of connection. They're not making mental notes of how many times the person says "I" or "me" but they know the message is inherently self-centered and not inclusionary in any way. They process that as a negative.

It's a simple guiding principle for you to follow: When you're a leader—or if you want to become a leader—the message always needs to be about "we" and "us."

Successes need to be shared. It's not about you.

There is one exception to this rule, and it shows true leadership. The only time you should use "I" or "me" is when something goes wrong. You're the boss and the buck stops with you, so rather than throwing other people under the bus, own it, take responsibility as the organizational leader. People know the company is more than one person but owning an issue takes strength and shows leadership.

Are You Bill or Raj?

From the very beginning, Bill's instinct was to be transparent about the tailings pond breach. But his communications manager was saying it was nothing to worry about. Bill isn't a communications expert but he assumed someone with a title like Communications Manager of a major mining company knew what they were doing.

Bill realized his manager was experienced at corporate communications like sponsorship deal-making, external affairs, marketing and writing a news release every now and then. He didn't have experience in the media nor in crisis communications situations. Now they were paying for it.

In the meantime, Raj was acting quickly. He was bringing in the experts without hesitation. After all, he's great at running a company but he was smart enough to realize that crisis communication is a very different skill set.

Takeaways

- DIY communications is as dangerous as DIY heart surgery.
- Lawyers are not professional communicators.
- Lawyers and boards have a fiduciary duty to the company, not you as CEO.
- Apologize quickly and often if an apology is necessary.
- Practice using the language of leadership.

Questions to Ask Yourself: When a crisis happens, who are the key non-media, non-crisis operation stakeholders you will need to communicate with quickly to ensure you set the narrative with them (i.e., regulators, politicians, staff)? Who will contact them and how?

CHAPTER 7

Buckle Up and Lead—How to Navigate through the Landmines

It was common to see an executive sitting in this dimly lit downtown Chicago hotel bar. But it was rare to see one like Bill—so shaken and chalky white.

Raj had a difficult time recognizing the man sitting across from him. Raj estimated his old friend had lost 20 pounds in a month. He certainly wasn't looking like a CEO, and that concerned Raj, who wasn't accustomed to seeing this man so broken.

The Gut Punch

"How are things?" Raj asked in a softened voice that was hard to hear in the crowded bar.

There was a long, awkward pause. Bill reached up to his forehead and rubbed the ridge right above his eyebrows.

"I'm done," Bill's voice cracked. "It's over. After busting my ass for over twenty years, I've had my reputation destroyed. I didn't even do anything wrong. I'm just the scapegoat."

"The tailings spill?" Raj knew the answer before he even asked.

Bill nodded as his stare shifted down towards his drink. He whispered, "Our stock price has plunged and the Board is meeting next week. There's more bad news coming, and it doesn't look good for me. Honestly, if I were them, I'd cut me loose as well and give shareholders their pound of flesh."

Bill had no idea how he would get a job after this. He was in his early 40s, and this issue was going to stain his personal reputation. He waited weeks to see Raj, to get some feedback and hear some insights. Bill was aware Raj had been doing a lot of proactive work in the area of issues management for his company, so there was much to share and learn. He was just hoping it wasn't too late for the advice.

They Don't Teach This in Business School

Raj ordered two more drinks. They were going to need them; this was going to be a heavy meeting.

As Raj returned to the table his phone rang. He set the drinks on the table and knowing exactly who was calling, hurried off to find a quiet corner to talk.

Bill watched him go. He knew what "Raj in action" looked like and this was it. Raj was upset. He was gesturing with his hands like the person on the phone was standing right in front of him.

It was only two minutes before Raj hurried back to the table. He was in a panic. Apologizing to Bill, he gathered his belongings and stuffed them into his satchel. He fumbled with his phone until he found a phone number in his contacts. He put a call through while Bill watched.

"Hey, Carrie? It's Raj over at Shlomo. Sorry to bug you. You know that issue we've been dealing with? It just got *way* worse. Can you meet me at the office in Boston first thing tomorrow morning? I'll brief you once I'm somewhere private."

Raj and Carrie spoke for a few moments before ending the call. He turned to his old friend. "That was my crisis person. Thankfully, she is on retainer with Shlomo. I'm so sorry, Bill, I need to go. That privacy data breach we had just got much worse. Can I call you tomorrow night?"

Bill understood completely, especially considering what he was going through with his own crisis. And, if he learned anything the hard way, it was to act faster sooner. He imparted that advice on Raj earlier and clearly Raj took that advice. Bill knew he had to continue this conversation soon with Raj to learn from what he experienced.

The two men shook hands and pulled into a hug. They went their separate ways, each wondering what they were in for.

Boston, the following morning ...

Carrie Boswick ran her fingers through her hair and stifled a yawn. It was 09:45, and she had been in the Shlomo office since 06:00.

Bavington had a rapid response team at the ready for clients facing a major crisis. As the project manager, Boswick had taken the lead. She had flown in from Washington the previous night. From the time Raj made the first call, she was wheels down in Boston in less than four hours.

Raj had actually beat Carrie to the office by about half an hour. He had been in the Shlomo boardroom since 05:30, but for the first half hour he made do with making coffee and assembling a list of stakeholders. He wanted Carrie to be there when they got to work. She was the expert.

For a couple of hours, he had focused on sending emails and making phone calls. He had learned there was no such thing as overcommunication when it came to key stakeholders.

Raj was tired, and a bit overwhelmed, but he was coping. He hung up the phone and allowed himself a quick minute to gather his thoughts. After rubbing his eyes, he called, "Next" to the person lining up his phone calls. He had spent all morning on the phone, calling everyone from the Food and Drug Administration to consumer organizations. The reception had been what Raj would describe as "open but skeptical."

Carrie had put together headline messages. The initial statement had been released to the public last night:

> We have learned a 19-year-old Shlomo client affected by last week's data theft has chosen to end her own life.
>
> Raj Thackeray, Chief Executive Officer, says the entire Shlomo team is taking the news hard. "Most of us are parents ourselves. We built Shlomo to help clients who are struggling with mental illness. We feel sick this has happened. We're going to do everything we can to prevent this from happening again."
>
> Shlomo has pledged our full and complete cooperation with the Boston Police Department in their ongoing investigation.

Acting on Carrie's advice, Raj committed to keep as many parties informed as he could.

Repetition Drives Retention

They had set up a basic website with a daily news update when the hack was initially revealed. They sent a copy of their statement to that email list and promised to share more as the investigation continued. In the meantime, Raj worked the phones. He closed his eyes and rubbed his fingers over the corners and said, "Carrie, it feels like I'm saying the same thing over and over again."

"That's because you are, Raj," she replied. "But that's not the issue. The issue is whether it's working."

Raj sighed and picked up the phone to make another call, this time to a medical reporter with a TV station in St. Louis, Missouri. The phone calls were very similar. Raj opened the conversation with a statement of genuine caring and concern.

That's when the questions started. Sometimes they were accusatory, like "How could you let this happen?" or "How do you feel about the fact you drove a young girl to suicide?"

Sometimes the questions were technical in nature. But no matter how loaded the question was, Raj was careful not to take the bait. He said a lot of things like "You've asked a question that means a lot to me," or "I've asked myself that same question."

Then he'd answer. And usually, no matter the question, the answer would boil down to, "We're doing everything we can to keep this from happening again."

There Are No Shortcuts

The company had the actions to back it up. They were conducting a full security sweep. They were taking steps to encrypt every computer. They had hired a third party to do a security audit.

The security specialists hadn't started but Raj reported they had been hired. And he committed to ongoing updates.

It was hard work. Raj was tired. He had been operating without sleep for close to 30 hours. But he felt good. People were upset, but no one was outright yelling at him or being abusive.

He hung up the phone with the St. Louis reporter and turned to Carrie. "I need a break. Can we work in an hour or two for me to grab a quick nap?"

"Hang on to that thought, Raj" she replied. She was turning up the volume on the television for the local NBC affiliate station.

The two of them watched a reporter outline some of the facts. It stung. The report over dramatized a few points a bit more strongly than Raj would have preferred. Interestingly, the station had asked for comment from the National Mental Health Association.

The NHMA spokesperson said "This is tragic. But it's important to remember people don't self-harm because of one problem. They self-harm because they're sick and need help. Whether it's a data breach, a nasty breakup or a death in the family, what's important is not to focus on the spark. Our focus is giving people the support they need to control the fire."

Raj blinked. He turned to Carrie. "That's actually pretty good for us, isn't it? I mean, we're doing everything we can after a screw-up to fix it, but here they are saying it wasn't malicious? That's good, right?"

Carrie nodded and started scanning for more contacts. "It *is* good. It's exactly what you need. Did you recognize the spokesperson? You met with him four months ago."

You're Always Being Watched

The last thing Carrie did was give Raj a handwritten note that outlined a short email to send to all staff, reminding them of their non-disclosure agreements and how that included not discussing company business off company property.

"What's this for?" Raj asked.

Carrie pointed out she was in the Starbucks next door before the meeting and overheard two staffers discussing the data breach in a public space. She said there was no malice—it's just that people have a false sense of privacy in public places, and a reminder email is probably a good idea during an issues management situation.

Raj agreed and typed out the short email and hit send.

Next …

Don't Make Room for Negativity

There are a lot of things that go through your mind in the first 12 hours of a crisis. Some of those thoughts are toxic. They will poison you, your company and your career within minutes.

Thoughts like:

- I don't deserve this.
- We can't say anything because we don't know anything!
- Why is everyone picking on me?
- I need a few days to make sure I'm doing the right thing.

Nothing good comes from those types of thoughts. There is no room for self-pity. There is no room for indecision. A crisis requires speed and a focus on solving the problem. "Making sure I'm doing the right thing" is not a substitute for "I'm afraid to say this because I'm afraid of the consequences." If you confuse the two, bad things are going to come your way.

There are also some good thoughts that can work into your brain. These thoughts are like gold nuggets found in tons of wet dirt. They're rare. They're easy to miss. But they're the reason you're sifting through the dirt in the first place; dive on those thoughts. Love them. Think about them time and time again.

Thoughts like:

- We can get through this.
- I know that if we do the right thing, this will pay off.
- I understand why they're angry. After all I'd be angry, too.
- This is going to be a valuable learning experience.

These are the sorts of things that are 100 percent true. But these thoughts are so fleeting, so whimsical, it's easy to ignore them or not even notice they're there at all.

The Story of Keith: How to Act Quickly Without Information

It was 12:04 pm when we got the phone call. It was Keith calling from his head office. Keith owned a hot-air balloon company in Portland, Oregon.

Keith didn't have a good idea of what the problem was, merely that there was an explosion and one pilot had been taken to hospital. We didn't know if he was alive, dead or somewhere between. That's a lot of incomplete information.

Being in a crisis is scary. It's chaotic. There's a lot of yelling. Emails and phone calls fly back and forth. Keith was in Canada and had a tough time speaking to staff on the ground in Portland, literally because of the sirens in the background.

But despite all that chaos, Keith had a spokesperson doing live television at 12:15 pm. From the moment the phone rang to the time we were on air—eleven minutes.

How on earth did we do that? We didn't have a lot of information but we did have some; and based on what we knew, we knew we had to act. There is *no* substitute for speed. Keith had access to a media-trained spokesperson because they had prepared in advance.

We were following a three-point messaging model, which works well in the first few hours of something severe and acute, meaning right here, right now. This could be something like a propane explosion, a fatality, or a natural disaster.

1. Tell what you know.

In this case, we knew there was a propane explosion, and that one employee was taken to hospital. Why was this important? It was important because Keith and his team could reassure people the giant fireball was *not* terror related. It was important because we needed to confirm our passengers were safe. This was an industrial accident, not a flight safety problem. We wanted to show that hot-air balloon rides are safe and this explosion has nothing to do with safe flights.

In fact, the explosion happened in a part of the facility that's not open to the public. That was good information. We could share that.

2. Tell what you *don't* know.

Keith's team was able to openly disclose that our pilot had been taken to hospital. We didn't know if he was alive or the status of his injuries. We didn't know why there was a fire in the first place. We didn't know how it started.

Why was it important to disclose that information? This one is even simpler. We knew it was going to be asked anyway. By anticipating the questions, you can answer them before they're asked. It allows the spokesperson to be in control of the conversation. We knew we would be asked about the pilot, so rather than go through the dance of questions and answers, we cut it off. We weren't going to even risk appearing defensive. It's better to preemptively disclose what you do *not* know.

There's no shame in admitting that you don't know everything. Open disclosures sets the stage for future authenticity and openness. Let's be honest, no one expects you to know everything right away. Most reporters know this but they're still going to ask, so surprise them. Be shockingly honest on the easy things and they'll believe you later on about the tough things.

3. Tell them where they can go for more information.

Sometimes more information is as simple as "I'll be back here at 11:00 pm to give you another update." If you tell a group of journalists "I'll be back at 11:00 pm," what time do you need to be back? If you answered 11:00 pm, you're already a couple minutes too late. There is zero room for error in a crisis, so if you tell people you'll be back at 11:00, show up at 10:58 pm and start proving you can be trusted and credible.

More information may be made available via your social media stream or a dedicated web page. Sometimes it's appropriate to refer questions to emergency first responders. But make sure people know where to go for further updates. So, taking the steps to prove you can be trusted and a reliable source of information is great because you'll need that credibility later.

Do you recognize the model? You may remember how Rudy Giuliani communicated during and after 9/11 (for a brief learning moment, forget some of the PR problems he has had since leaving office). He was widely praised for his clear communications at the time. During 9/11, what citizens heard was essentially a version of:

- **What we know:** "We know that the two World Trade Center towers have been brought down. Several buildings in the complex are damaged beyond repair. I can confirm that we have lost everyone on Engine 54 and Ladder 118, along with countless others."
- **What we don't know:** "We are still waiting on status reports from most of our crews. We have a list of known survivors. If you would like to add your name to a list of survivors, you can do so by going to this website address. We do not know who did this. I do know that the City of New York will offer any help we can to the agencies investigating."
- **Where to go for more information:** "I'll be back at 11:00 pm with a further update."

Sounds familiar? Giuliani was praised for how he communicated through the 9/11 terrorism attacks, and for good reason.

Make Room for Action

Let's take a quick moment and talk about leadership. If you're in a crisis, this is not the time for democracy. Crisis demands leadership. Crisis demands action. If you insist on running your communication decisions past a committee, you may as well use that time to print your resignation letter.

Crisis communication demands military-style assured command. It's rough, bumpy, and it's not comfortable. If it were comfortable, everyone could do it. This is a defining moment that separates leaders from followers. Which one are you going to be?

Remember ... lack of speed kills careers.

Buy Time with a Rapid Response

There are going to be times you don't even have the time to put together a detailed script. Still, do what you can to follow the model. It will buy you time.

A simple tweet that says, for example, *"Refueling explosion at facility on Atkins Drive. One pilot taken to hospital. No passengers involved. Stay tuned for updates at 2pm"* does a few important things for you, not the least of which is buy you time. It allows you to figure out what is going on and what you need to be doing next. Maybe there's a statement you can share via social media (albeit with more words) or a quick news release or email. But at least acknowledge the issue and buy yourself time.

It may only buy you an hour or two. But at least the talk of the town is not going to be about terrorist attacks, dead passengers or exploding balloons. Even a hold of a few hours allows you to shut down the damaging rumors and innuendos before they even start. It's called "feeding the beast." The beast is the media. Look, you know they're going to be talking about you. So, give them something to talk about. Make sure the information is accurate, won't damage you, and allows you to fashion a more considered response.

Now, in those few hours or so of bought time you can gather a lot of information but you need to be ready to feed that beast. And, in Portland, we knew we needed to feed that beast, so we had Keith's people doing live television within eleven minutes.

It worked. The media learned and the public accepted this was an industrial accident. That's not to say it wasn't serious or we weren't taking it seriously. But we can say it wasn't terrorism and it had nothing to do with passenger safety.

The Federal Aviation Administration called Keith the next day. He was open and honest, and he forwarded several news articles. When they were satisfied it was not a flight safety issue, they closed the case that very afternoon. That's an important endorsement. It allows us to say that we're still flying passengers as soon as we get replacement equipment.

Replacement equipment was brought in from all over North America. The balloon company even had competitors offering baskets, trucks, balloons and equipment. We decided to take advantage of the media and public interest. Eleven days after the company lost all its equipment in a massive fireball, we invited the media on our first balloon ride back. We made sure to bring the pilot, who had suffered some burns to his leg and shoulder but was otherwise fine.

The TV stations went live from the hot-air balloon basket. The newspaper did a story and included a video on their website. Most importantly, ride sales didn't decline at all.

Eleven months later, Keith sold the balloon company for a tidy profit.

It's Not the Party that Hurts—It's the Hangover

Keith's story shows the importance of getting holding information out quickly to feed the news beast before it feeds on you. But what comes next?

Just about anyone can handle a crisis in the first few hours. But careers are made and careers are destroyed by how they answer "How" and "Why."

We call them the Monday Morning Questions (even when they're not asked on a Monday). Just as a quarterback from a football team playing on Sunday will have his plays analyzed and picked apart on Monday, so will the communicator in a crisis. Monday Morning Questions will come at you hard: "Why did your tank explode?" "Why should we fly with you?" "Why should we believe you when you say your balloons are safe?"

How do you move on from here? How do you calm down the skeptics who want to pick apart every move you make? Ultimately, you're looking to come up with something that will allow people one simple fundamental point: You want them to *trust* you.

Trust is critical. Your audience may not like what you have to say. They may not like you. But they can still choose to trust you. Trust is what turns angry hordes into happy repeat clients. Trust is what calms activist reporters. Trust is what can convert a judicial investigation into a polite phone call with a request "not to do it again."

Trust is the engine oil that lubricates the motor of commerce. Without trust, that engine will go nowhere.

How to Gain Trust in the Middle of a Crisis

So how *do* you earn trust in the middle of a crisis? That's a question countless clients have asked us. The fact is that only a minor part of the answer are the words you speak. Instead, it's more about how you say the words, everything from body language, voice tonality, inflection, and pacing. Do they believe you? Do they trust you? Are you credible?

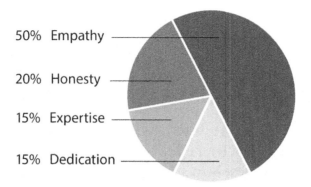

Professors at Columbia University have studied this complex equation:

- Honesty is worth 20%.
- Competency is 15%.
- Dedication is 15%.
- Empathy is 50%.

These figures show that even if you are the world's leading expert on an issue, your knowledge is only a small fraction of what regular people judge you on.

What is this empathy superpower that accounts for half of the audience's interpretation of the message? Empathy is the ability to understand and share the feelings of other people—your audience, whether that's your investors, clients, employees, the public, neighbors or regulators. Crisis communications is all about being empathetic and validating how people feel during a challenging time. It seems easy but it is easily the one factor the majority of CEOs forget about in a crisis, and the end result looks cold and inhuman.

Emotions will usually override facts. That angry horde of reporters, customers or regulators are trying to communicate how they feel. Unless you have a way to tell them that you can feel what they're feeling, they will keep trying to show that to you. And you're not going to like the ways they communicate.

Emotions mean that instead of an angry phone call, you get sued by upset clients. Emotions are why protestors show up outside your headquarters. Emotions are why angry letters are written to the editor. Emotions are why regulators subject you to investigations. Why do politicians get belligerent and throw you under the bus? They're communicating how they feel.

It does not matter if you're correct. It doesn't matter if you have facts on your side. It doesn't matter if other companies did even worse things. If your board has to choose between firing you and facing months of angry editorials and lawsuits, what will they choose?

Formulating Empathetic Headline Messages

Thanks to effective messaging, Raj was able to deliver empathy. He did this by using a headline message, the very essence of what he was trying to communicate. A headline message is a "thud statement." It stands on its own and can't be argued with or misinterpreted.

Statistics show that up to 80 percent of people read the headline, not the story. What do you want that headline to say? Does this mean the local newspaper will use your statement as their headline? No, of course not. We can only strive for that. But we're going to do everything we can to get there.

Raj's headline message was, "We're doing everything we can to keep this from happening again." He didn't try to defend his corporate practice or pin the blame on the thieves. He could have tried to do that but he would have ended up playing defense instead of advancing his agenda. Your headline message will change based on the circumstances around the crisis. But no matter the circumstances, an effective headline message always has three characteristics: brevity, positivity and honesty.

1. A good headline message is brief.

Raj used 11 words. It shouldn't be longer than that because it is, quite literally, a headline that would appear in the newspaper or on the crawling scroll on the all-news TV channel or the tweet the media sends out. Headline messages are short for two good reasons. We want them to be "sticky" in people's brains. The shorter and more pointed a headline message is, the more impact it has on your listener.

Brevity is your best friend when it comes to social media. Remember, your audience is likely not hearing your headline from you. They're reading about it on Facebook or Twitter or hearing about it from their Great Aunt Sally. The shorter and punchier your headline is, the more likely it is to be repeated verbatim. And that's exactly what you need in a crisis.

2. A good headline message is positive.

This isn't the time to deny negatives with further negatives. We want to tell our audience what we are, not what we are not. For example, Bill Clinton could have said, "I've conducted the office of President with integrity and honor." That's a lot less vivid than "I did not have sex with that woman." Negatives are considerably more memorable than positives. People won't hear the word "not" or "don't."

When you use a negative headline message, you're repeating your worst attributes and making them more memorable. This is why "Our hot dogs won't make you sick" is a lousy headline message. "Nothing is more important than the safety of our customers" is a great headline message.

3. A good headline message is true.

None of what we're talking about here works if you're spinning a lie. Never lie. You need to honestly, in your core, believe you're doing the right thing. Can you say that nothing is more important than the safety of your guests? Do you mean that? Are you prepared to fight for that? Make your case with fervor, humility and authenticity. Go and speak authentically. Speak from the heart. And do it again, and again, and again. We saw this with Raj, making phone calls directly to his important stakeholders. If that sounds intimidating, well, we're not going to lie to you. Hell yes, it's intimidating. It should be intimidating. This is the future of your career at stake, if not the future of your company.

Loose Lips Sink Ships

This wartime message warning people against giving information away to the enemy is relevant here. Don't let your media strategy get scuppered by careless conversations in public spaces. We can't tell you how many times we've been in a coffee shop and overheard businesspeople talking strategy—information that should only be discussed in a boardroom. As journalists, we would intentionally hang out in diners and coffee shops near a company and listen in on the conversations, looking for information to act on.

Despite what you may think, you have no reasonable expectation of privacy in a public place, whether it's a restaurant and coffee shop or a park, street corner or beach. Even the garbage you put out on the street corner is fair game for people to pick through if they want. Courts have frequently ruled that people have no expectation of privacy regarding things they do and say in public.

And, it's not just actions that get captured. Sometimes it's people's own social media activity that gets them attention. Some seem to forget that many social media posts are public conversations. We can't tell you how many times we get called in to undo the damage caused by something someone says on Twitter.

Let us drive it home with a blunt force object: don't say or do anything in public that you won't want to show up on the evening news or front page—or even worse, on the internet. Social media is way less forgiving than journalists.

Repetition Drives Retention

In our ongoing parable, you see a lot of the same principles. Raj acted fast, because he had Carrie to help him get through a bunch of the mental hurdles. But that wasn't all Raj had going for him. Raj also had effective headline messaging.

In a crisis, you may get sick and tired of repeating yourself. But you know who won't be sick and tired of hearing from you? You know who wants to feel empathy? You know who wants to know that you're honest, telling the truth, and know what you're doing? Those are the people you are communicating with. Your audience.

You see this with Raj. He was communicating to an audience. That audience was looking to him for reassurance and *wanting* to trust him. What if you were in Raj's shoes? Do you have an audience that needs to believe you?

If you get tired of honestly portraying your truth, it means you may be doing it right. It's hard work but it's much simpler with the help of a trusted guide to help you every step of the way. This is not stuff you want to try to do on your own.

Takeaways

- Feed the media fast. Buy yourself time in order to think clearly. But respond quickly.
- Focus on empathy, empathy, empathy.
- Words matter. What do you want your headline to say?

Questions to Ask Yourself: In a crisis, who on your team will be monitoring the media and social media in real time? Who will be responding to messages and taking calls from reporters?

CHAPTER 8

The Power of a Mob

As Bill struggled with his crisis, he couldn't help but think about the movie *Gladiator*. Back in the days of Roman gladiators, thousands upon thousands of people gathered in a single location. Like a social media mob today, the Roman era mob was powerful. They had the power to decide the fate of both the gladiators and their own rulers. The rulers knew this and feared the mob.

In *Gladiator*, Russell Crowe's character, Maximus, had become a slave gladiator and was fighting for his freedom. His master, a freed former gladiator named Proximo, gave him this advice: "Win the crowd and you will win your freedom." His meaning is that the mob dictates the actions of the politicians.

Nothing had changed since Roman times. Bill was learning that. Bill realized he needed professional help with this crisis even if it was months too late.

While the rapid response team was neither rapid nor responsive, the public pressure surrounding the tailings spill hadn't stopped nationally. It was given oxygen by environmental groups who had joined forces with Native American community leaders. They staged a protest in

Washington DC. For the environmental groups, incidents like this are great ways to raise awareness for their causes. They tend to attract big donations from rich, older benefactors looking for a head start into Heaven. Bill was begrudgingly impressed by the ability of the environmental groups to stay on a simple message, connect on a human level, control the agenda and keep the pressure mounting.

In this case, Nevada media were getting bored of the story, so the special interest groups moved the story to Washington DC. For the Capitol Hill media, who grow tired of covering the same old thing every day, this was a refreshing change of narrative. It was a story they hadn't approached from a political perspective. It was a new angle. As an added bonus, when it gets covered in Washington by the big networks, it breathes new life into the story back home. Many local reporters at home want to be network reporters and the Washington coverage validates the legitimacy of the story. So, it becomes a bit of a self-fulfilling prophecy in some respects.

Back in northern Nevada at the spill site, everything was now contained. The tailings pond was rebuilt better than ever, but in terms of water quality, there were elevated levels of arsenic. It certainly wasn't great. However, independent water quality consultants reported the issue was being mitigated. There would be limited long-term impacts on wildlife and no impact on humans. There have been way worse environmental mining disasters in recent memory. Again, this wasn't great but it wasn't horrible.

But none of that mattered.

You had arsenic in water, and to the majority of people who don't understand science, this was very bad. When is arsenic good?

And now you had it making news in Washington. The narrative had unfolded over months to the point where the company's name was a reputational liability. Bill and the company had stopped doing interviews and were only responding by lawyer-approved email statements. It was a bunker mentality.

The worst of it came on the regulatory front. Where previously Bill was assured these were acts of God and an investigation was routine, it now seemed as though the story was changing. The public pressure was having an impact on local, state and federal politicians of the region. They were getting attacked on social media and, thus, in the media for being too pro-industry.

Stories had come out showing the company had made political donations to a number of politicians. Although a normal way of doing business in American politics and perfectly legal, the optics were horrible. And it put pressure on politicians. Bill had lost the support of the mob and they were giving a collective thumbs down.

The company was getting fewer updates from the EPA. The tone was changing. Investigators were coming back for repeat visits with more specific questions each time.

Meanwhile, the company's Board was having in-camera meetings, which is never good if you're a CEO under fire. The Board Chair said he had called an emergency meeting and they wanted Bill there. It was to discuss "strategy and the future of the company." Stock prices were plummeting, investors were pulling away and now the real pressure was that politicians were getting on board with the activists. To make matters worse, charges appeared to be forthcoming.

The meeting was short and sweet. The Board questioned the $200,000 expenditure on a crisis communications company at a time when they were having major cash-flow issues. That said, they'd give Bill a pass on it as it was an operational issue. Then the big revelation came. The very consultants Bill hired met with the Board Chair and he asked them only one question: what is the fastest way out of this?

Bill was given a generous severance package, a combination of cash and stock options intended to incentivize him to say nice things about the company as he would have liquid investment in it. For additional safety, they locked him down with an iron-clad non-disclosure agreement. No discussing his departure. No discussing the reasons why. No discussing the money. Even when the inferred public narrative would be that he was the problem and the problem was now gone.

Bill never saw the crisis company again but he did see their work in a well-crafted news release that went out the next morning that outlined the departure. The quote from the Board Chair was the real beauty:

> "When Bill was hired, the Board knew he didn't have a mining background. We felt at the time his financial experience was what was needed given the changing face of the commodities market. We accept responsibility that it was a failed experiment on our behalf. We have engaged a firm to initiate a global search for our next CEO with the clear directive it has to be someone with mining experience. We wish Bill the best in his future endeavours."

What Happens When You Get Ahead of a Story

In Boston, meantime, Raj was having a completely different experience.

When the breach was first discovered, Carrie had a holding statement written and approved by the legal department and the Board within hours. Now, with this unfortunate suicide, Shlomo was ready. It was proactive and ready to handle the challenge.

For Immediate Release
Media Statement

Shlomo CEO Promises to Do More to Protect Sensitive Data

(Boston, MA) On behalf of Shlomo, our Board and our employees, I want to express our most sincere condolences to the family of one of our clients who, we have learned, has taken their own life. We are so sorry to see a young person with so much promise think this was their only way out. I have personally reached out to the family and spoken to the parents to share our feelings.

Earlier this year, as we proactively disclosed to the public, we suffered a theft at our headquarters that led to a data breach of some of our client information. As a company that deals with sensitive information, I can say we're doing everything we can to prevent a data breach from occurring again. While I cannot speak about any specific client for privacy reasons, we can confirm that the only information breached involved names, addresses and credit card information. No case file information was breached.

Shlomo has hired a third-party security firm to complete the review of the breach. They have already initiated protocols to ensure the highest levels of encryption technology, as used by the Pentagon, so that human error will not happen again and all data is safe. I'll say it again: We're doing everything we can to prevent a data breach from ever occurring again.

Mental health is a major global crisis. More than 120 people take their lives in the United States each and every day. These are our spouses, our parents, our siblings, our children, our work colleagues, our neighbors and strangers we pass on the street every day. The fact is, in one way or another, we have all felt the impacts of mental illness.

At Schlomo, we are helping tens of thousands of people via our online support program by connecting them to licensed therapists in all major fields based on individuals' specific issues. Therapy can be expensive and challenging to get appointments. This is why we created Shlomo: To make mental health crisis support more accessible.

Having a mental illness means you are sick, not weak. We encourage anyone who is having thoughts of self-harm to contact the National Suicide Prevention Lifeline at 1-800-273-8255.

For more information:

Raj Thackery

Raj@Shlomo.com

The Media Blitz

The media release went out immediately and Raj did a series of interviews, including with journalists he met during his outreach tour with Carrie. He also reached out to key stakeholders he had relationships with to brief them on the unfortunate incident.

A memo went out on the app and website to all Shlomo clients. It encouraged them to use the tools available to them through Shlomo and public resources when in extreme situations. It had a primary focus on ensuring no copycat suicides were triggered—that everyone was safe.

Later that week, Raj was in the office when his COO tapped on the door of his office. "You're not going to believe this," she said, "but, in the past few days, since the crisis happened, we've had over 5,000 new clients register."

The story had been covered nationally. Initially, Raj felt guilt about the fact they had seen an increase in business through a crisis. So, he walked down the hall to the office of Janice, Shlomo's Senior Technical Advisor.

She was the company's head of therapy, basically. A licensed psychologist with over thirty years experience, she was the brains behind the service. Raj briefed her on the increase in clients and how that made him feel.

"That's 5,000 people with mental health challenges," Janice pointed out. "Last week, they had no support. Now they have us. How is that a bad thing?"

It had been a long day. Raj thanked Janice and headed home.

Speaking of mental health, when he got in his car, Raj realized Bill sent him a text hours earlier saying he had been fired. Raj wasn't surprised. It had been a long, painful ride for Bill, and Raj tried to be there for him as much as he could. He'd call Bill when he got home.

However, it was at that point that Raj realized how incredibly lucky he got by being ready for the crisis storm. At the time, it was hard to justify the expense, but as he saw how it played out for Bill, there was simply a sense of relief. Life is funny that way.

The Truth about PR

This is a good time to point out a special secret in our industry.

Some people call it "PR," short for Public Relations. However, that is a very broad umbrella description. PR is just a huge toolbox, but it is the specific tools inside that box that you want when you're facing a communications crisis.

In your situation, you don't need a PR agency that does marketing and outreach, and not even a media relations consultant. You need a specialist, someone who does crisis communications and has a lot of experience in the field. They must have experience they can draw on quickly to help you in your situation.

We got into this to help people. Making money is great, but we like problem-solving. Many of the good crisis experts come from journalism, a trade that is high on advocating for people and low on income. We love the power of truth. We love persuading. And we love winning. We are addicted to the adrenaline involved with working a crisis. That's the difference between specialists and broader PR agencies. With specialists, there are usually no "junior" people. And they're only as good as their last client's success.

That experience is what differentiates crisis experts. Gray hair means something in this business, where speed of response matters, and speed is predicated on drawing on years of experience-based strategies and tactics. Before hiring your crisis communications person, ask very specific questions like: What were the top three crisis situations you personally managed? What has been the main challenge you've faced, and how did you overcome it? Ask them what the last crisis situation was they worked on. But if in telling these stories, they identify who they worked for, run away as fast as you can. You want someone who practices discretion. And, finally, if you are meeting with a big agency, ask who specifically will be managing your crisis hands-on if something happens? Who is that person and what kind of experience do they have?

The Scapegoat Strategy

The scapegoat play isn't a new one, as any experienced lawyer or crisis strategist can tell you. We have been in the situation with clients of being asked by the Board of Directors what the fastest way out of the fire would be. And, although we're not human resources consultants and would never recommend terminating someone, when asked a specific question about the best way to protect the reputation of the organization, the answer is often to "give the public their pound of flesh." The person who is terminated often gets a huge financial payout; however, the optics of being the problem that required a solution lingers long after the money runs out.

Why does this matter? What message are we sending you? Well, it is vital to remember that CEOs come and go, but the fiduciary duty of the Board is to the company and the shareholders/investors. Their loyalty is NOT to any one individual.

When a crisis hits and the storm is coming hard, often the fastest way out is cleaving the CEO from the herd, publicly, and letting people make assumptions regarding blame. This is why you, as a leader, need to be detailed, proactive and diligent in ensuring you are ready for a crisis that hasn't happened yet.

You *need* that trusted third-party advisor who can step in immediately to protect your back. Someone who knows what they're doing. Someone who is neutral enough to tell you bad news to your face. Someone who knows you, knows your media market, knows your industry and most importantly, knows how to get you out of a crisis. There are many experienced and talented crisis communicators out there. Find one, develop a relationship during peace time, agree on rates, and be ready.

A Side Word about Apologies

In order to actually apologize, you need to do three things.

Actually Say You're Sorry. Saying you're sorry can go a long way in putting a mistake behind you. Not "I was wrong" or even "I apologize." Say the words "I'm sorry" multiple times. Make sure the public hears you saying it. It takes multiple times for it to sink in. Saying you're sorry doesn't mean you are admitting guilt or liability -- it can simply mean you are sorry the incident happened. Do make sure it is cleared by your lawyer to ensure you have not admitted liability.

Be Sincere. Authenticity and sincerity can only come across in your nonverbal communications—meaning your body language and voice tonality. In other words, you either have to be the best actor in the world or you must truly mean what you're saying. It's impossible to fake. People are perceptive. It takes practice and professional coaching to make it work effectively.

Make No Excuses. It's not "I'm sorry, BUT …" If you're going to own it for the purposes of moving on, then own it. Apologize with no excuses—repeat and repeat again. If you are unable to authentically apologize without excuses, we would recommend going with a written statement. It's not the ideal situation, but letting someone who can't give sincere apologies be the apologetic face of an entire organization is like leaving a three-year-old with sharp knives. A written statement isn't perfect, but it won't do as much damage as an inauthentic apology.

Raj Fell Up, Bill Just Fell

Raj created the conditions for victory; Bill was just checking off the box. And you can see the difference in the results.

Raj is falling up. He's going to weather the storm with increased credibility, increased trust, increased profits and, most importantly, more people are going to get the help they need with mental health issues. That's taking a tragic situation and truly falling up.

Bill is simply falling. His career is in tatters. He's unemployed and his reputation is ruined.

Takeaways

- Win over the mob and you'll win your freedom.
- Investors, boards and politicians are influenced by public opinion.
- Engage crisis specialists before a crisis. Make sure they'll be there for you.
- Anticipate issues before they happen. Work on mitigation strategies.

Questions to Ask Yourself: Once you have your crisis protocols in place, where can people find them, wherever they are when the crisis hits? Who is responsible for updating the protocols quarterly?

CHAPTER 9

The Aftermath

Several Months Later

Bill came around the corner and could see his cottage just around the bend. He accelerated his pace and broke into a sprint for the final 100 meters, breaking the imaginary finish line at the telephone pole by the corner. He checked his watch: right on pace. He'd been doing the 8k run every day for the past three months now.

Breaking pace, he peeled his t-shirt off, chugged down half a bottle of water and collapsed on the grass. The sun was already high in the sky, and it was nice to sit back and recover in its warmth. He was lying there, catching his breath, eyes closed, when he felt a shadow fall across his face.

That's when he heard, "Thanks for the show, buddy, but I'm not stuffing dollar bills down your shorts."

Bills eyes snapped open. "Raj! What are you doing here?"

"I'm in town. I tried to call but I had your old work cell. I called Helen and she said you were on your run. I thought it would be good to drop in and see you."

The two sat down in a couple of Adirondack chairs on the porch. Raj looked at his old friend. "Okay, so the jokes about the shirtless show aside, you look good. Last time I saw you I was worried."

The two caught up on life for the past several months. As it turns out, Bill wasn't quite marched out of his offices in Colorado, but it was close. He was only given a few hours to clean out his personal effects and leave the premises. In the words of Nicholas, the Board Chair, "A clean break is better for you and it's better for us."

Bill wasn't surprised when the axe finally fell. He cringed as he relayed the story of going home and walking through his front door, box in hand. His wife, Helen, walked around the corner, surprised to see him home so early. When she saw the box, her eyes fell in instant recognition of what happened.

Rather than moping around Denver, Bill decided to spend a few months away. An old friend had a property in the Chesapeake Bay region; the perfect place to decompress for a few months.

"Any opportunities coming down the pipe?" asked Raj.

"I've had a few nibbles. I'll land on my feet. It may not have as much cachet as CEO of the most rapidly growing mining consortium in the Southwest, but, hey, life goes on. What about you? Why are you in town?"

Raj explained that, actually, he made a detour to swing up and visit his old friend. He was in DC to pick up a "Mental Health Heroes Award," an award given by a consortium of mental health advocacy organizations.

Bill was suitably impressed. "That's major. You were just trying to make your way around the medical technology industry a couple years ago. Now you're getting industry awards?"

"Yeah. I get it. But I think it's mostly Carrie's award." Raj explained that the data breach was scary for everyone, but it had an upside of thrusting

Shlomo's technology into the spotlight. Raj was profiled in industry publications all over the globe with headlines that asked, "What is Shlomo, anyway?" The profile and public attention gave them a lot of exposure. The share price had initially taken a tumble but within a few days had recovered completely. Then it started to climb.

Shlomo had a great meeting with the family of the girl who took her life. Raj even flew to the girl's hometown to meet with the family. Her parents were sad but genuinely impressed at the care Raj was placing on the issue. They even ended up saying, publicly, that they supported what Shlomo stood for.

The glare of the spotlight faded away and mainstream media moved on to the next story. Carrie had returned to her office at the Bavington Group. The "traditional" communications department had taken over, now that the crisis was over. With the increased attention, they arranged several feature stories on new Shlomo technology. Shlomo even had some celebrities publicly talk about their experiences using the app.

The attention was fantastic. Shlomo had started as a boring experimental research firm. Today, they were leading the charge on drug-free solutions to mental health problems. Raj was pretty optimistic for the future.

"I'm so happy for you." Bill said. "I have to admit, when you left the bar in Chicago, I was concerned I'd never see you again. That's a pretty tough card to have been dealt. You were pretty shaken up."

"Yeah, it was a lot of work. But I had some great help," Raj replied.

Bill looked down. "Yeah. This kind of challenge was way too important to do on my own. I learned that the hard way."

Raj slapped his hand on his friend's back, then made a show of disgustedly wiping off the sweat. "Look at the bright side. You're in shape again. For now."

Which Kind of Leader Are You?

Here's a confession: We didn't want to write this book. We have clients, families and things to do. Plus, let's be honest, there's no money in books.

We wrote this book because good people and good companies are having their reputations maligned without a proper defense. They are either trying to get through it themselves, relying on inexperienced staff, or depending on some expensive templated crisis communications plan that sat on a shelf collecting dust. These CEOs and companies are in dangerous waters and have no real defense in the court of public opinion. We want to raise awareness and open people's eyes regarding best practices.

Here, you read a tale of two nearly identical corporate leaders, with two very different results.

One relied on an old-school, traditional crisis communications plan. He ended up unemployed. The other focused on active, ongoing preparation and capacity building in the event of a communications crisis. And he's now picking up industry awards.

Take a look at your own communications team. They're probably fantastic at what they do, Monday to Friday, when it comes to writing news releases, designing brochures or writing a speech. But do they have the skills *you* need when you get the frantic phone call at 03:00?

Our hope is that you'll stop what you're doing, right now, and take a look at your own operations. Take a look at your own crisis communication plan. Go over and look at it and see how long it takes before you find information that's missing, incomplete or already out of date. We bet it won't be long if you have one at all.

We've asked you a series of questions throughout this book. If any of them gave you pause, we want you to consider your next steps.

Three Easy Steps to Take Right Now

There are three things you, as a leader, can do right now that will put you in a dramatically better position. They hardly cost a dime but they can save you millions in future liability claims, and they just might save your career.

1. Line up a trusted third party.

Crises aren't solved by writing them down in an old-school crisis plan. Crises can be solved by having someone you trust tell you exactly what to say, how to say it, and to whom. That person can't be someone on your internal team; it needs to be a person who's not going to react emotionally because their office is on fire. A trusted third party—an expert who knows how to stomp out a crisis—is invaluable for any corporate leader. If you don't have that person in place, figure that out and formalize that relationship immediately.

2. Create your crisis protocols.

While an old-school crisis communication plan tells you what to say, your crisis protocols are much leaner. You don't need to know exactly what to say or to whom (you've got a trusted, third party advisor for that), but you *do* need to know things like "who's your spokesperson?" What's the best way to communicate if our system has crashed? Or Where will we assemble if our building burned down?

The good news is that assembling your crisis protocols isn't difficult. It's absolutely not worth paying a consultant tens of thousands of dollars to create. In fact, if you want a template of effective crisis protocols, we'll happily email you a set for free. Simply visit www.LeadersUnderFire.biz. Filling in the blanks will help you immensely.

3. Get you and your spokespeople trained.

Crisis communications training is a gift that gives *before* you find yourself in crisis. The ability to talk to an upset investor, calm them down, and have them leaving happy will pay for itself ten times over. Imagine if you knew exactly what to say to a nervous regulator *before* they decide to release a damaging inspection report?

Plenty of companies can offer media training but be careful. You don't want vanilla "media training." That will be helpful when you're doing a TV interview to launch your newest product but it won't help you when CNN wants your comment on a damaging headline.

We've put together a one-page "Things to look for" brief on how to find a good crisis training solution. We've included some questions to ask and an idea of what to budget. It's yours for free at www.LeadersUnderFire.biz.

Conclusion

Like we said in the introduction, the story of Raj and Bill is a parable based on a collection of true stories. We have sat in the boardroom and helped corporate leaders become absolute heroes of their community after a crisis. And truth be told, we've also been the ones who have recommended that a company fire their CEO.

We've sat through data breaches, natural disasters, industrial accidents and untimely deaths. We've seen the best and the worst.

We encourage you to go get the free tools we've offered you - the crisis protocols and the "Things to Look For" brief. Send us a note to let us know if/how it helped, or what you'd like to see from us that would make your lives as CEOs under fire even easier. We hope to hear from you.

Made in the USA
Monee, IL
14 February 2020